COLLECTOR'S GUIDE
COMIC BOOKS

Wallace-Homestead Collector's Guide™ Series
Harry L. Rinker, Series Editor

COLLECTOR'S GUIDE TO
COMIC BOOKS

JOHN HEGENBERGER

Wallace-Homestead Collector's Guide™ Series

Wallace-Homestead Book Company
Radnor, Pennsylvania

Copyright ©1990 by John Hegenberger
All Rights Reserved
Published in Radnor, Pennsylvania 19089, by Wallace-Homestead Book Company

Designed by Anthony Jacobson
Manufactured in the United States of America

Library of Congress Cataloging in Publication Data
Hegenberger, John.
     Collector's guide to comic books / John Hegenberger.
         p.   cm.—(Wallace-Homestead collector's guide series)
     Includes bibliographical references.
     ISBN 0-87069-548-7
     1. Comic books, strips, etc.—Collectors and collecting.
   I. Title.   II. Series
   PN6714.H44   1990
   741.5′0973′075—dc20   89-51561
                                                                 CIP

2 3 4 5 6 7 8 9 0   9 8 7 6 5 4 3 2 1

To

Julie, Stan, Gardner,

Murphy, Joe, Jack, Mike,

Carmine, Gil, Wayne, Curt, Kurt,

Dick, John, Steve, Milton,

Chester, Will, Neal,

Frank, and Mom

Contents

Foreword

While it is difficult for today's comic-book fans to believe, a quarter of a century ago it was extremely hard to find comic books for sale. There were no comics stores, and the number of newsstands and drugstores carrying comic books was constantly dwindling. Few stores—fewer all the time—deigned to waste space on comic books.

The only comic books you could find on a reasonably dependable basis were those in the Archie line. A lot of newsstands and drugstores continued to carry those because parents bought them for their children.

The hardest comic books to find were Marvel Comics—even Charlton Comics were carried more widely than Marvels. Marvel was a minor company. Almost all of the stories were written by the editor, Stan Lee, and almost all were drawn by one of a handful of staff artists, including Jack Kirby, Steve Ditko, Don Heck, and Gene Colan. Occasionally, Al Williamson would draw a Western story or Jack Davis would illustrate a fantasy story.

All of Marvel's comic books were poorly printed. Legend has it that they were printed on Charlton's presses; I must confess that I have never checked this report because I might find out that it was not true—and it's such a nifty twist that I want it to be true because Marvel is today the undisputed giant of the industry and Charlton was always the least of the comics publishers. Marvel comic books were seldom found in "mint" condition, even on the newsstands. The presses did such a shoddy job of trimming the copies that there was shredding along the edges and frequently there were tiny pieces missing along the edges of at least some of the pages and particularly on the covers; collectors today call these defects "Marvel chipping" or "Marvel chips."

I started buying Marvels when Marvel started publishing stories about superheroes, starting with the first issue of *Fantastic Four*. About a year after that first issue of *Fantastic Four,* Marvel was also publishing the adventures of Spider-Man, Thor, Hulk, Iron Man, and Ant-Man—half-a-dozen comic book titles in all. In order to buy one copy of each of these, I had to check newsstands in four Ohio cities: Cleveland (where I worked), Elyria, Lorain, and Oberlin.

Twenty-five years ago, comics fandom was just getting started, and its voice was only faintly heard. The number of collector publications in the field was small and of limited circulation, and collector opinions had little influence on what was published. That was understandable, in view of the tiny percentage of comic-book buyers who could be considered comic-book fans or collectors. There were *maybe* as many as 5,000 comics fans—not enough to influence the editors of comic books with a circulation in the hundreds of thousands.

The *idea* that anyone would own a store which sold *only* comics and comics-associated items wasn't even a dream for anyone I knew. I was still desperately trying to locate a newsstand which actually carried Marvel's then-current comics.

Of the three newsstands in Oberlin, where my wife Maggie attended college and where we lived for the first two years of our marriage, only one carried any Marvels. Only one carried *Classics Illustrated* issues, which were still being displayed. Dell comics were still coming out, and Dell's takeover by Gold Key was still in the future. There were Archies, and Charltons, and—of course—there were DCs. But no newsstand made any attempt to carry all the comics; there was limited space on those newsstands, and, once the racks were filled, any comic books left over were returned to the distributors without ever being displayed for sale. Marvels were sent back undisplayed more often than any other company's titles because they had not yet built themselves an audience.

Marvel's first issues were especially hard to find. Today, when the hottest collectibles are generally first issues, it's hard to imagine that there was a time when publishers tried to avoid publishing first issues. Once the available rack space was taken, the store clerks looked for something to remove to make way for proven sellers. What went back most often were first issues—why put an untried title on the rack instead of something that had already lasted a dozen issues or more?

Publishers tried various means to get around the first-issue stigma. Often a title would be changed with the numbering continued from the old title, no matter how radically different the two titles and their contents were: E.C. Comics changed titles several times and attempted to keep the numbering (sometimes the Post Office made the company change its numbering, but sometimes E.C. got away with it), resulting in *Gunfighter* becoming *The Haunt of Fear*. In another case, E.C.'s *Moon Girl and the Prince* became *Moon Girl*, which became *Moon Girl Fights Crime*, which became *A Moon . . . a Girl . . . Romance*, which became *Weird Science*.

Some publishers went so far as to start each new title with #5 or #7. Collectors went nuts for years trying to find early issues of titles which had never *had* any issues earlier than #5 or #7.

Marvel entered the superhero field cautiously, except for its initial venture. *Fantastic Four* began with #1 and featured four new characters, only one of which had an established name—The Human Torch—though he bore no direct relationship to the Golden Age hero of the same name. (Golden Age comics are those published from about 1933 through the late 1950s; comics published from the 1950s through the 1970s are Silver Age comic books.) The Incredible Hulk was also introduced in his own title, but he was not an instant success; his comic book was canceled after only six issues, and Marvel editor Stan Lee proceeded more cautiously. Thor was introduced in the pages of *Journey into Mystery* and eventually took over the title. Spider-Man was introduced in *Amazing Fantasy* #15 (the last issue of that title) and was given his own title only after all the sales figures were in.

All of these things happened without the benefit of organized fan newspapers and magazines to tell comic-book fans what was coming up. Collectors had to hunt for everything—and a lot of adult collectors felt they had to pretend they were buying comics for their kids.

It was not "in" to be an adult who collected comic books.

To be sure, there were advantages to collecting comic books in the 1960s. For one thing, the competition was not so heavy and the prices were a lot lower (though, for some of us, it was as hard to come up with a dime in 1965 as it is to come up with a dollar in 1990).

Comic-book stores began when collectors set up a shop to sell, buy, and trade comic books to improve their own collections. The earliest of these were operated out of the basements of the collectors' homes, but some of them went on to rent small stores. In addition to selling the duplicates from their own collections and buying the collections of others, they tried to carry new comic books as well.

No discussion of the current state of comic books is complete without mention of Phil Seuling. Phil changed the way comic books had always been sold and enabled what had become a marginal business to survive and thrive.

Comic books—like all other magazines and like paperback books—are sold to newspapers, drugstores, and other outlets on a returnable basis. That is, the store buys them from distributors at a discount and sells as many copies as it can. The ones the store cannot sell are returned to the distributor for credit—or at least the covers or part of the covers are returned—and the distributor returns them to the publisher. With this method, it takes a long time (about six months) to get final sales figures—which leads to the cancellation of a lot of titles after six months. It also means that a publisher must produce more than twice as many copies as it sells, and the newsstands have to carry more copies than they sell.

Phil persuaded the comics companies to sell comic books through distributors directly to comic-book stores for a bigger discount, the advantage to the publisher being that these direct-sale titles would *not* be returnable. It was the responsibility of the store owner to assess how many copies of a given issue of a given title the store's customers would buy. It was *not* to the store owner's advantage to carry more than he or she could sell, whereas a newsstand could carry 50 or 60 copies, sell only five, and return the covers of the remaining 45 or 55 copies for credit. With the new system, the publisher did not have to overprint a title.

The direct-sales system had the added advantage of making it possible to make a profit on a comic book with a smaller print run, which in turn made it possible to target a specific audience—including an adult audience—with a new title. This gave the comic-book industry a wider range of titles than it had enjoyed since the 1940s. It also made it possible for publishing a comic book to become a cottage industry—you could write and draw a comic book in your own home, find a printer, convince a distributor to carry it, and make money on a circulation of just a few thousand copies. There were cases of teenagers saving their allowances and their lawn-mowing and paper-route money, publishing comic books they created themselves, and—at least for a while—making a tidy profit.

The big comics companies found themselves with real competition for the first time in years in the form of companies with names like First Comics, Eclipse Comics, Comico the Comic Company, and Eternity Comics. However, Marvel and DC Comics also found themselves making vastly more money than before. Comics writers and artists, traditionally able only to eke out a meager living, were suddenly able to make a good living, often six figures a year.

All this and more came from the efforts of Phil Seuling. Phil didn't have long to enjoy the fruits of his labor. He died of a liver ailment less than a decade after his efforts had created the direct-sale market and had, in the process, saved the comic books he loved.

Comic-book collectors everywhere owe him a great debt, one they repay every time they visit a comic-book store. The existence of comics stores makes it a lot easier to be a comic-book collector, and those of us who remember what collecting was like before the comics stores will always appreciate Phil's efforts.

Collectors have always needed all the help they can get, which is one reason why John's book is welcome. Experience may well be the best teacher, but the tuition can be painfully high—and it's possible to learn from other people's successes and mistakes, which is a lot cheaper. This book lets you avoid the common mistakes and find the successes of comics collecting.

Don Thompson
Iola, Wisconsin

Acknowledgments

I am indebted to the following people and companies for their kind consideration in developing this book:

The publishers and editors of DC, Marvel, Eclipse, E.C., First, and Kitchen Sink comics—the kinds kids like;

My two-fisted editor, Harry L. Rinker, and the world's finest publisher, the late Alan Turner;

80-page giant John Stingley for his excellent photography;

All-stars Don and Maggie Thompson for their years of devotion and leadership calculated to drive you to collect comics, madly;

The uncanny Richard Wright, Gloria Morgan, and Ro-Z Mendelson, for local insight;

My wife, proofreader, and pal, Suzie, and my marvel family.

Introduction

When I first started collecting comics, there was no one to show me the way. No one to tell me where to find comics, how to store them, or who would ever want to trade or buy them. Fortunately, this is not the case for the collector today.

Collector's Guide to Comic Books is a passport to greater fun and entertainment in the fascinating world of comics, but it is also a useful handbook for the investor and speculator. This guide will tell you the best way to find and buy old and new comics, how you can organize and take care of them, and finally, how to go about selling what you've collected so that you can go out and collect *more* comics.

Yes, it's possible to make a profit collecting comics, but it's equally possible to get burned by making a bad investment in the comic-book marketplace. Most collectors want to know what their collections are worth, which comics will become runaway best sellers, and how much money can be made by buying wisely. Some serious collectors realize several hundreds or thousands of extra dollars each year by purchasing and selling comics. Why shouldn't you?

Collector's Guide to Comic Books is jammed full of good advice, useful information, and "secret" tips that will help beginning collectors—and even experienced pros—expand their collecting powers and abilities far beyond those of normal collectors. Despite its great value, the information presented is not hard to understand, for it's based on common sense. By reading this book, you'll learn how to make your collection grow without risking your life savings.

The primary purpose of this guide is to help you maximize your fun and enjoyment. I remember the surge of adrenalin that ran through my veins when I saw my first comic collection years ago. While I was visiting a friend he pulled open a drawer of his dresser and presented me with the sight of stacks and stacks of old and strange comics. These comics featured dozens of "new" adventures of my favorite characters and included "lost" episodes of their colorful lives, complete with loads of excitement, action, and

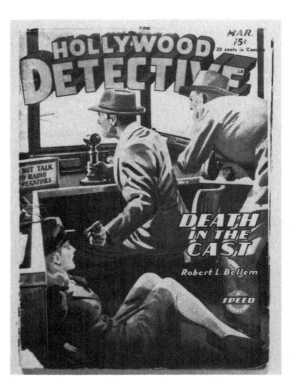

Fig. I-1. *Hollywood Detective,* March 1946. One of the few pulp magazines that enhanced its content with the use of comic adventures. (© Speed Publications)

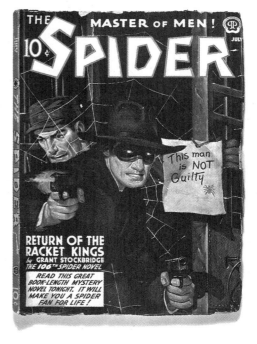

Fig. I-2. *The Spider,* July 1942. The pulp magazine was the father of the comic book in form and content. Here's a masked crime fighter many consider to be tougher than Batman. (© Popular Publications)

Fig. I-3. *Fiction Illustrated* presents *Chandler*. In the mid-1970s various attempts were made to expand comics beyond their traditional formats. What is remarkable here is not the book's smaller dimensional size (5″ × 6½″), but that this independently produced, one-shot comic survived in the marketplace away from its typical youth audience. (© Byron Preiss Publications)

Fig. I-4. *Wanted #9* with Victor Everhart. Crime comics went so far as to create the impression that their readers could assist the police in identifying and capturing wanted criminals. (© Lev Gleason Co.)

Fig. I-5. *Crime Does Not Pay #53*. Lev Gleason's "crime" comics of the late 1940s led the way to the E.C. line of the 1950s. Not only were the stories "all true," but note the subtle use of sex and multilevel visuals in this book's cover. (© Lev Gleason Co.)

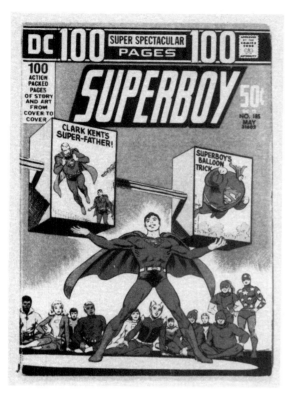

Fig. I-6. *Superboy* #185. In the early 1970s, DC Comics provided a bargain in its 50-cent, 100-page books that relied heavily on reprints. These books are still an inexpensive way of gaining a look back at important comics history. (© DC Comics)

intrigue. That was the moment when I knew I wanted to collect comics, and a small piece of that moment comes back every time I get a new book for my collection.

For most people, the inspiration to collect comics isn't so startling, and the collecting instinct isn't so sharp. If you're like most people, you slowly realize over the years that these multicolored pamphlets of daring adventures and light amusement seem to pile up around you. You read and reread them (sometimes to pieces), and you pore over the artwork. You never consciously set out to collect comic books, but it just sort of happens.

And keeps happening, because comic books are part of our childhood history. Right now, somewhere, another new collector is discovering comic books for the first time, because comics are everywhere and they appeal to just about everyone. They're a clever and artful combination of words and pictures, writing and drawing, literary and graphic arts. Sales of comics in the United States during 1988 topped $250 million. Over 100 million new comics were sold nationwide. More than 5,000 special comics retail stores currently serve millions of customers daily. And nearly every comic ever printed is available today to you through the wide network of collectors and dealers.

Clearly, comic books are all around us. You can buy them at bookstores in a mall, or at your neighborhood comic-book shop. You can get them directly in the mail from the publisher, or you can subscribe to one of many high-volume discount services. You

Fig. I-7. *Lois Lane* #115. In the late 1960s and early 1970s, the limits of the Comics Code Authority were being tested on all fronts. It seemed at that time that every month one character or another was encountering death. (© DC Comics)

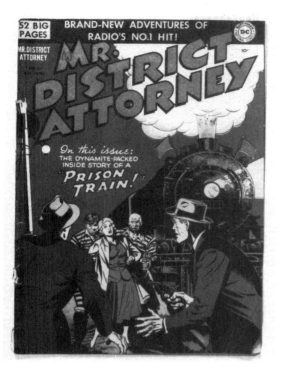

Fig. I-8. *Mr. District Attorney* #15. Popular radio crime drama like *Big Town* and *Gang Busters* found a ready audience in the comic readers of the early 1950s. (© DC Comics)

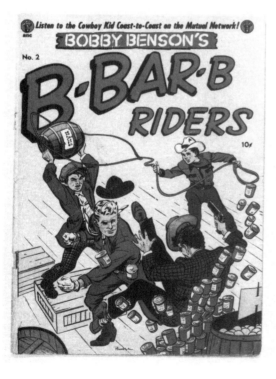

Fig. I-9. *Bobby Benson's B-Bar-B Riders* #2. Mutual Broadcasting's *B-Bar-B Riders* combined kids with cowboys, and a comic-book adaptation was not far behind. (© Magazine Enterprises)

Fig. I-10. *Star-Spangled Comics* #115. Many frontiersmen, like Davy Crockett and Daniel Boone, found a ready audience in the comic books. DC Comic's Tomahawk character saw over 20 years of publication. (© DC Comics)

Fig. I-11. *Superman* #115. Due to the popularity of the "Superman" television series in the 1950s, DC Comics found Superman to be its most marketable character. This was the first comic owned by the author. (© DC Comics)

Fig. I-12. *Ken Shannon #6.* Horror was so popular in the early 1950s that it even found a home in private-eye comics. (© Quality Comics)

Fig. I-13. *Mad* #35. In order to survive the negative repercussions of the Comics Code, William M. Gaines moved *Mad* comic over to create *Mad* magazine. This issue emphasizes the publication's Mad-ison Avenue aspects. (© William M. Gaines)

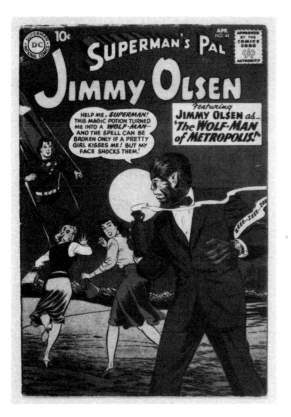

Fig. I-14. *Jimmy Olsen #44.* Horror movies of the 1950s meet Superman's pal—a winning combination for its time. (© DC Comics)

can trade them with your friends, or you can swap them at any of the comic conventions held throughout the country every year.

But it didn't used to be this way. Comics began as a humble selling tool for Sunday and daily newspapers (early ones were *Famous Funnies* and *Comics on Parade*). Then a few enterprising printers saw a need for reprint volumes of the most popular strips as a way of keeping the presses rolling and the money flowing in.

This was the *Golden Age* of comics in the United States (1933–1959), when comic books found a ready audience in children and members of the armed forces. Within 10 years of the creation of comics it seemed that anyone with a printing press, a pen, and an imagination was producing them. Comic books were perfect for flights of fancy. They were a lot less expensive than movie special effects, yet almost as convincing. Back then, comic books let readers vicariously travel the universe, performing mighty feats—for just a dime.

But all this illustrated daring and violence worried a generation of adults who'd fought for peace during World War II and dreaded the threat of the nuclear cold war. A world full of hope for tomorrow is what Americans sought for their children in the 1950s, and after a while comics became regulated in content to reflect these ''wholesome'' ideals. At that point, the Golden Age was over.

Fig. I-15. *Fear #1.* Before there was a Spider-Man, Marvel Comics filled the newsstands with strange characters like Goo-Gam, Son of Goom, and Monstrom. (© Marvel Comics)

Fig. I-16. *The Brave and the Bold* #35. The Silver Age of comics began with the revival of many DC Comics heroes from the 1940s. Here's Hawkman as he looked when he returned to comics in the early 1960s. (© DC Comics)

However, the roots of the *Silver Age* of comics were just taking hold. From 1959 to 1968, American comic books rose like the heroic phoenix rising from its ashes. A whole new host of adventurous superheroes, many of whom were clever revivals (like Captain America) or updated versions (like Hawkman) of their Golden Age counterparts, leaped from the pages of comic books, bringing more realistic science, relevant issues, and detailed backgrounds into their readers' minds.

Superheroes became married and started families. Teams of them broke up as important characters quit the trade, or even died. This period in the history of comic books was dominated by three publishers: Marvel Comics, DC Comics, and Gold Key (Dell) Comics. Also during this period readers began to discover one another and to communicate using homemade comics and fanzines. Comics fandom was thus born, and things were never quite the same again. People were serious about collecting, and comics quickly became "big business" again.

The years 1968 through 1978 represent the *Iron Age* of comics. During this time Marvel and DC generated dozens of new titles, nearly exhausting themselves to gain the majority of the readers' attention. Major comic conventions began to take place annually all over the country. Professional fanzines started appearing. Comics became a workhorse, with hundreds of monthly titles cascading week after week from comics outlets. At the same time, collectors and distributors initiated the first direct-sales organizations

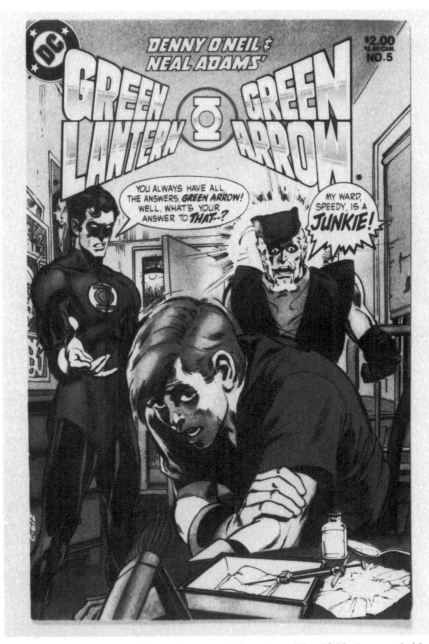

Fig. I-17. *Green Lantern/Green Arrow* #5. Comics of the 1960s began taking on more relevant subject matter in order to maintain their maturing readership. (© DC Comics)

Fig. I-18. *Fly #12*. The publishers of Archie Comics prided themselves on their entry into the field of superheroes in the early 1960s. The Fly was a hero who had the powers of a—fly. (© Archie Comics Group)

and comics shops, through which new and old books and related materials were bought, sold, and traded daily, like commodities on the stock exchange.

Thus was born a whole new industry. Dozens of new comics companies came into being almost overnight (such as First, Eclipse, and Pacific, to name three), ushering in the current *Chrome Age* of comics, typified by slick covers, glossy stock, bright inks, international reprints, and classy, hi-tech marketing through stores in shopping malls all across the country.

Collecting comics is now one of the world's most popular pastimes, probably because in addition to just *collecting* comics, you can also *read* them. And in addition to displaying comics, you can develop a literary and artistic appreciation for their many writers and artists. And you can even turn a profit with comics, if you're careful.

Maybe you collect comics for the love of them, or for the memories they bring back to you, or because you enjoy a certain artist, or because they take you to an alternate reality with strange characters in unusual exploits. Maybe you collect them because they represent a quality investment. Your reasons for collecting and the makeup of your collection can tell you something about yourself, and that, too, is a good reason to collect.

There are three fundamental types of collectors: the basic collector, who loves the wonder, the art, and the characters; the collector/speculator, who has a prize collection

Fig. I-19. *Cartoons Magazine,* February 1915. Long before the invention of the comic book, *Cartoons* collected the pen-and-ink illustrations of political cartoonists from around the world.

Fig. I-20. *Tales of the Teen Titans #50.* By the mid-1980s almost everyone in comics was getting married; so much so, you could hardly tell the heroes from the villains, or the characters from the creators. (© DC Comics)

Fig. I-21. *Twisted 3-D Tales* #1. Today's horror comic, plus 3-D. (© Blackthorne Comics)

Fig. I-22. *Captain America* #250. A superhero for President? It almost happened in 1980, but an actor was elected instead. (© Marvel Comics)

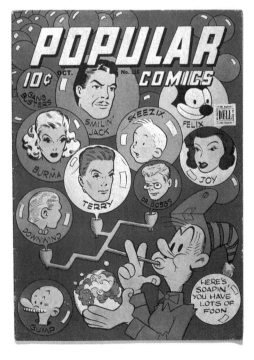

Fig. I-23. *Popular* #116. Newspaper strips collected into comic-book format; an example of the sort of comic book popular in the late 1930s. (© Dell Publishing)

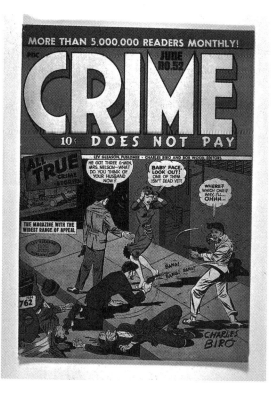

Fig. I-24. *Crime Does Not Pay* #52. Post-WWII crime comics were direct and to the point. The kids loved it. (© Lev Gleason Co.)

and a few extra books set aside for swapping and dealing to expand his or her collection; and the investor/dealer, who know the value of rare and important comic books and makes money transferring comics from person to person. (These "types" are discussed in more detail in Chapter 9.) *Collector's Guide to Comic Books* is appropriate for all three levels of collecting. It's the book you need to help work your way through all the collecting activity: the conventions, the shops, the hype, the choices, the fun, and the excitement.

This book has developed slowly over the past several years, partly as a result of my own experience and partly from interviews and discussions with people who've bought, sold, traded, collected, and produced comics since the late 1960s. I saw a need for a book such as this because I found, over and over, that much of the important nuts-and-bolts information that collectors needed simply wasn't available to them. I found, also, that some of the information used widely among collectors was inaccurate, misleading, or downright false.

Because of the enormous amount of activity in this field, plus all the new comics published weekly, *Collector's Guide to Comic Books* will need to be updated from time to time. If you have any suggestions for additions or improvements I would like to hear from you by mail. Please write to me in care of Wallace-Homestead Books, Chilton Way, Radnor, PA 19089.

It is my hope that you'll find this guide to be an invaluable aid to your collecting skills and enjoyment.

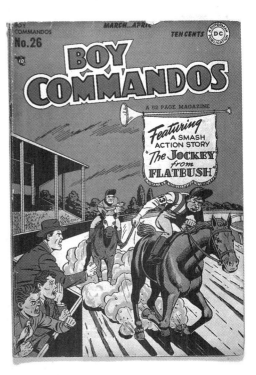

Fig. I-25. *Boy Commandos* #26. After WWII, heroes did practically anything to find adventure. (© DC Comics)

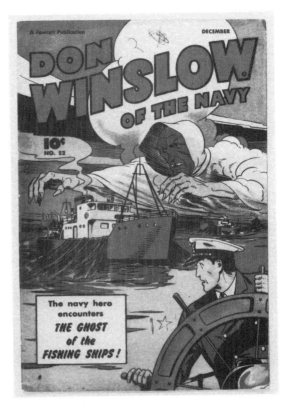

Fig. I-26. *Don Winslow* #52. After WWII, readers required comic stories that stretched beyond everyday criminals and Nazis. Here's an early example of a horror theme appearing in a straight adventure comic. (© Fawcett Publications)

Fig. I-27. *Classics Illustrated* #124 is an example of pictorial literature often used for book reports (instead of the actual book!) in the 1950s. (© Gilbert Publications)

CHAPTER 1

Approaches to Collecting Comics

MY FIRST APPROACH TO ORGANIZING MY COMICS was to file them by the title and number of each issue. Then, after about six months, I had great fun going back and re-sorting them all and filing by date. Because comic books are numbered, the traditional system for organizing them is "by the numbers." But the "by the date" system has its own advantages, too.

When you sort out your books by date, placing all the January cover-dated books together, you can see what happened in the world of comics at a specific point in time. Perhaps your favorite character, say, Superman, "crossed over" into another title that month to appear in Wonder Woman's book, or perhaps the entire summer was filled with one long and rambling adventure that wove its way throughout a comics company's entire line. (In 1989, Marvel Comics had several of these "events" running at the same time.) By sorting your comics by date, these sorts of larger story lines can be revealed and relived just as they happened.

There are many other ways to collect, as well. Most collectors prefer to collect by title; that is, they collect one particular title, like *The Avengers* or *The Revengers,* and try to get every issue, plus annuals, special issues, and graphic novels (see Glossary) that are published under that title. If you collect that way, it is almost certain that when you buy the next issue of your chosen title you'll get a book you'll enjoy.

Other collectors go further in this process and collect by character; they might not only buy every comic published under their character's title, but they might also make a point of getting every book, regardless of title, in which their favorite character appears. For instance, if you like Spider-Man, there are a lot of issues of *Marvel Fanfare* you'll want in your collection, because he often appeared in that line, too. Since you have selected a character that you like to read about, if you collect this way you're going to enjoy your collection—while getting exposure to some other titles you might enjoy in the process. (This is the publisher motive for those long and rambling adventures.)

Fig. 1-1. *America's Best Comics* #27. Here's a comic-book cover within a comic-book cover. This type of "infinity cover" is a popular collecting subcategory among many collectors. (© Standard Publications)

Fig. 1-2. *Big Shot* #96. Christmas themes on the cover of comics are a popular and valuable subcategory for many collectors. (© Columbia Comics Group)

Many people collect by artist or writer; that is, they might buy every book that Frank Miller or Paul Chadwick draws, or every book that John Byrne or Mary Wolfman writes. This is particularly appealing to the collector who enjoys the art of comics as much or more than the characters themselves; it allows a collector to see how a comics creator has developed skills over the years and exposes the collector to the variety of characters and concepts that the creator has handled.

A few collectors try to collect all the books produced by a particular company, but unless you choose a very small company, this approach can get very expensive very quickly. Also, remember that ''company identity'' means a lot less than it did a decade or two ago, during the Silver Age and the Iron Age; creators may now be working for many companies at the same time, and you might miss out on some material you'd like to collect, just because it didn't have the right corporate name on the cover.

A few collectors make a point of collecting every first issue published. This collecting approach can also get very expensive. Furthermore, while the idea is a noble one—if you choose to pursue this course, it will expose you to every book being published, and you will know what everyone is doing—it can also fill your collection with a lot of books you don't enjoy while burdening your budget.

Another way of collecting that is related to first issues is specialization in origin issues. *Origin issues* explain the origin of a character—how he or she got started and gained his or her powers. For the comics historian, origin issues are the most desirable. However, origin issues do not exist for every comic-book character. Some creators of comics characters never bothered to construct origins for them. When a character is introduced in a comic without his or her origin being told, the particular issue of the comic is called an *introduction issue*. (A final note on origin stories: Origin stories are so popular that publishers sometimes retell or rerun them.)

Finally, some collectors specialize in either time period or comic type, preferring, for example, to collect comics only from the 1960s or those with horror titles. Since comics have been around for almost 60 years and have dozens of types (western, war, crime, love, funny, animal, and so on), this sort of collection can include any subclass or any combination of categories. DC once published *Weird War Stories* and E.C. Comics published a comic titled *Saddle Romances*.

Since comics are almost everywhere, there is no problem acquiring books for your collection. Rather, there is a problem of too many comics, too many decisions, too many ways of collecting comics you may not want. Because there are so many comics to choose from, you need to be selective.

What's the best way to pick a comic for your collection? Easy—pick one that you know you like. Look over every comic you buy before you buy it and ask yourself a few questions. Do I want to keep this comic or just read it? Is it a special issue, or is it just average? Sometimes a comic won't even seem average, and in that case you already know you don't care for it, so why buy it?

Many people buy a comic just to have a complete run of a title. This gives them a clearly defined target, as they know from the outset how many comics are needed for completion and, roughly, what the cost will be. But having a complete run means some-

Fig. 1-3. *Major Inapak the Space Age #1.* Unique comics were used to promote products. This example is a highly entertaining space adventure produced in 1951 to help sell a chocolate milk additive.

thing only when you're ready to sell, and even then you'll encounter far more people who want individual issues from your collection, rather than a complete set. Most potential buyers won't be able to afford your entire collection of a title, anyway, and in many cases they have already been collecting long enough to have gathered together a majority of issues and want to buy only the ones they haven't seen before. In any event, there's very little financial incentive these days to owning each and every issue of a title, so collect only the ones you find interesting and leave the others for someone else.

The only good reason you might want to fill in the gaps in your collection is to follow the narrative adventure and watch as the characters change or grow. This means you're not actually buying by the numbers, but rather you're collecting comics because you like the stories and you want to watch as an adventure unfolds.

In the long run, *collect what you like* is probably the most important advice in this book. The popularity of a specific comic or character is sometimes only a fad. Popularity may spring from the right combination of creative talent, or just from the excitement and hype of a newly released motion picture. Whatever the reason, today's best sellers all too often have a way of becoming tomorrow's bombs. So, it's not always a good idea to buy your comics expecting that someday they will make you rich, because it may never happen.

But, if you collect what you like, you'll have hours of enjoyment regardless of

Fig. 1-4. *Wartime Romances* #2. In attempts to expand their market, many comics publishers combined popular themes, sometimes creating unusual story lines. (© St. Johns Publications)

fluctuating prices and the whims of popular taste. Hey, it's your collection, right? Why not collect what you want, instead of following the numbers or the crowd?

In addition to collecting comic books, there are several related items of interest to the comics fan. These include original art, Big Little Books, newspaper strips, gum cards, and foreign comics, each of which is described below.

Original art is the actual drawings created by an artist for production into the finished comic. Usually these are black-and-white pen-and-ink drawings that are later shot by a camera and converted into the printing negatives and plates used to print the finished work. Another form of original art is a sketch or drawing created by a professional while appearing at, say, a comic convention. Either way, a piece of original art is a one-of-a-kind item, and therefore highly prized. Owning a piece of original art is like owning a piece of comics history, and having original comics art framed and hanging on the wall can be a real thrill.

Big Little Books (BLBs) were a form of comics produced back in the 1930s and 1940s. For a BLB, comics from a newspaper strip or from a completely original series of drawings were assembled into a palm-sized book with hard covers and sold at local newsstands and toy stores. BLBs featured many of the famous comics characters of the day in complete adventures (some as long as 300 pages), with a panel of illustration on every page opposing a paragraph or two of story. Compared to the prices of old comics from the same era, BLBs are surprisingly affordable.

Newspaper strips are the original form of American comics. The earlist comic books were not much more than reprints of newspaper strips. Some collectors still clip and save the daily and Sunday adventures of their favorite characters. The real trick of collecting old newspaper strips is locating them. Few comics shops deal in them, and because of their loose format, strips tend to be difficult to read and handle.

Fortunately, in the last several years there has been a growing trend toward reprinting the more famous of the many newspaper strips. It seems the classics never go out of style. One thing to remember about the strips is that they appeared in the newspapers, alongside features appealing to many adult interests, while comic books of the same era targeted a much younger audience. Thus, by today's standards, many old newspaper strips have a quality and content equal to that of current comics. For instance, it was not unusual for a newspaper-strip character to get married and raise a family, something even the majority of today's comic-book heroes still have before them.

Gum cards are a variation on the familiar bubble-gum baseball-card format. Some gum cards feature comics or scenes from TV adaptations of famous comics characters such as Batman, the Green Hornet, and Superman.

Foreign comics can be a real treat. The trick is finding them, because foreign comics are of course produced outside the United States. Tracking down foreign comics is worth the effort, however, because seeing a familiar character handled in a translated version can be a "trip" in itself. In addition to finding that some basic adaptations of American comics are produced in foreign countries, you'll also find that the concept of the comic book has in some cases developed, mutated, and grown to reflect the cultures of the countries themselves.

Fig. 1-5. Big Little Books were collections of newspaper strips and were much like early comics except in format.

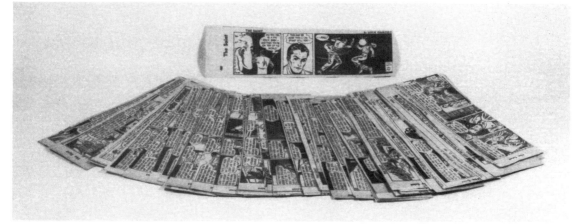

Fig. 1-6. A collection of newspaper dailies that have been carefully clipped and sequenced.

Almost every country in the world produces some type of comic book. If you have relatives or friends in other lands, you might ask them to send you a sample of their local comics. I guarantee you'll be surprised at the differences in size, content, and design of foreign comics. Having a few in your collection can give you insight into how flexible and functional the comic format is, regardless of cultural differences.

Other comics-related items you may wish to check out are toys, portfolios (see Glossary), posters, buttons, animation cels, (see Glossary), and even videotapes. For some collectors, comics are only the beginning, for others they are more than enough. In either case, comics are perfect for collecting.

CHAPTER 2

How To Get Started

NOT TOO MANY YEARS AGO, I could go down to my corner drugstore each week and spin the wire racks that displayed a welcome host of new comic books. Dozens of new and different titles appeared every Thursday in my town, and yet in one respect all of these different comics were very much alike. They were all approximately 6″ × 10″ in size and consisted of 36 pages of rag paper stapled together under a glossy cover.

There was never any question or doubt about the format of a comic book. You could spot one from across a crowded barber shop or doctor's waiting room by its size and shape alone. And when you bought one, you knew exactly what you had: three or four exciting stories for only 10 cents.

This, however, is no longer the case, for today's comics have blossomed into just about every size, shape, and price range imaginable. You can buy hardbound volumes of both classic and/new stories; ''prestige-formatted'' books with high-gloss laminated covers and more than 50 pages of quality paper and ink; books made from Mondo paper and Baxter paper, high-quality acid-free paper that will last a lifetime (see *Mondo paper* and *Baxter paper* in Glossary); graphic novels with European-style perfect-bound spines and oversized pages; paperback books; coffee-table volumes; boxed sets; annuals; special issues; and magazine-sized comics—as well as the old standby, the humble original comic books of 36 pages.

All this variety tends to delight and confuse today's collector. Obviously, the comics industry is attempting to reach out beyond its traditional format. But are the more expensive versions of comics necessarily better than their low-cost cousins? Is the art any better? Are the stories? You really don't know until after you've bought the book and read it, right? Unless, of course, you have a more experienced source of information that will tell you beforehand what's good and what's not.

Where can the new collector find such a friend? How can you safely get started collecting in this busy world of comics? Beyond this book, I can think of five other places you can go to get good advice and learn more about comics and comics collecting: other collectors, the library, the local comic-book shop, the comic convention, and collector publications.

Other Collectors

The easiest way to find out more about comics is to spend time with other collectors and fans. Look around your hometown for a local comic-book club where you can trade, buy, sell, and talk about comics. If there isn't one in your area, why not start one by placing some announcements on the bulletin boards of your local supermarket or library? It's possible that your school, church, or library would be happy to donate space for regular meetings of your comics club, and you can begin to share experiences with others who enjoy reading and collecting comic books.

The Library

The library is a super place to read up on your favorite hobby. There you're sure to find lots of books on the subject and perhaps even a reprint volume or two of the more famous comic stories and strips. Oftentimes, an inter-library loan will net you more material than you could read in a month of Sunday sections. And don't forget the microfilm files of old newspapers as a source for famous early adventures of old favorites like Superman, Batman, and Flash Gordon.

The Local Comic-Book Shop

Almost every major city in the United States hosts at least one comic-book shop. Check the Yellow Pages in your area under ''Retail Bookstores'' and ''Used and Rare Books,'' and do this whenever you visit a new city, as time permits.

A beginning collector can get a good education in collecting comics just by spending a few hours in one of these stores. There you'll be able to meet other comics collectors and get to see all the new comics that have just come out. You'll also be able to look over back issues and discover titles you never knew existed.

Most important, you'll be able to buy books, magazines, and newspapers devoted to comic-book collecting, as well as supplies for your hobby, such as storage boxes and bags. You'll get a chance to talk with other collectors and people in the business of selling comics, so you can ask questions and get lots of valuable information while making friends.

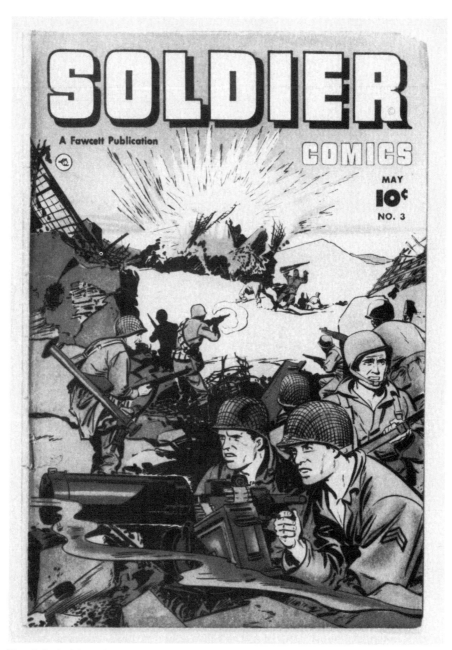

Fig. 2-1. *Soldier Comics* #3. The Korean War created a wide audience for adventure stories that recalled the battles of WWII or reflected the contemporary conflicts of the early 1950s. (© ACG Comics)

Fig. 2-2. *Saint* #10. Avon Publications brought out reprints of the *Saint* novels in the early 1950s and reprinted the character's newspaper adventures at the same time in comic-book form. (© Avon Publications)

Of course, comics shops are also excellent places to buy new and old comics and, usually, you can sell or trade books there, too.

The Comic Convention

A comic convention (also called a "comic con") is the absolute best place to learn about comics, but you've got to be alert. There's a lot going on at a comic convention, and it's almost too much for any one person to take in.

At a comic convention you will see thousands of old and rare comics available for sale and for trade. You'll meet other fans and collectors who share your interests. Sometimes, you'll even get to talk to the artists and writers who create comics and learn what's going to happen soon to your favorite comic-book character. You might win a door prize, get an autograph or sketch from a professional writer or artist, watch a slide show, or listen to a panel of professionals talk about what's happening in the industry. And you can buy, sell, and trade comics for as long as the convention goes on.

Comic conventions are held once or twice each year in most major metropolitan areas. There are local, regional, and national conventions held in almost every state.

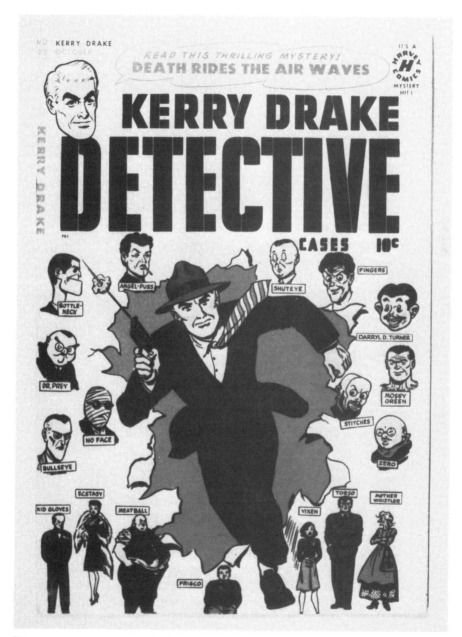

Fig. 2-3. *Kerry Drake* #22. The Kerry Drake newspaper strip also made the transition to comic books. Here Kerry bursts out of a cover surrounded by the images of his many bizarre villains. (© Harvey Comics)

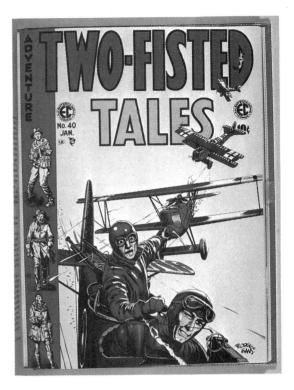

Fig. 2-4. *Two-Fisted Tales #40*. The first realistic war comic. (© E.C. Comics)

Major shows occur each year in New York, Chicago, Atlanta, and San Diego. Finding out about conventions is easy. Just ask the operators of your local comic-book shop, or check out the listings in the comics magazines and newspapers. Most of the conventions are held during the summer, but on any given weekend there are more than a dozen such gatherings taking place across the country. (The comic convention is *so* important that Chapter 7 of this book is devoted to that subject alone.)

Collector Publications

The best way to understand what's happening in the comic-book world is to read regularly several of the monthly magazines and weekly newspapers that focus on collecting comics. These publications can be purchased at your local comic-book shop or subscribed to by mail. They usually feature news, letter columns, articles, ads, and important listings on upcoming comics and conventions. From these publications, you can develop a feel for the current comics marketplace and a sense of history for your hobby. You can see which new comics are selling well and which old comics are available to fill in portions of your collection.

Some of the publications you'll want to look for are *The Comic Buyer's Guide, The*

Fig. 2-5. *Spirit* #1. Will Eisner's famous newspaper strip found a home for its reprints at Kitchen Sink in the 1980s. (© Will Eisner)

Fig. 2-6. *The Adventures of Superman* #424. Superman starts over. In the late 1980s, DC Comics revamped its entire line of superheroes in order to adjust to contemporary standards. (© DC Comics)

Comic Journal, The Comic Book Price Guide, and *Amazing Heroes.* For a complete list of publications and other resources, consult Appendix A and the Bibliography at the end of this book.

So, now you see how easy it is to get started collecting. There's lots of help available all around you (some of it free). Now all you have to do is find and buy some old and new comics and soon you'll become a seasoned collector.

CHAPTER 3

The Best Way To Find and Buy New Comics

AS A COMICS COLLECTOR of great experience, I can tell you that there was a time when I wanted it all. There was something vastly satisfying about the idea of owning and reading every new comic as it came from the publisher. Years ago, when comics were a dime apiece, this was not an unreasonable dream, but today's variety and multi-dollar price tags make buying even one copy of every new comic almost impossibly expensive. For the past few years, you would have needed to spend several thousands of dollars annually to reach this goal, and that's without spending a cent on back issues or related items.

There *are* several ways you can buy new comics without breaking the bank. The most fundamental and essential rule to good buying is to *never buy on impulse*.

In order to guard against that feeling of "Oh, I've just gotta have it!" that makes you spend over your budget, you should make a want list and a buying plan that you know you can afford—then stick with it. A want list will help you remember which back issues of a title you need to complete your collection. A buying plan will help you remember which new comics you want to be sure to purchase while at the same time keeping you on budget. Believe me, I know how easy it is to be pursuaded by arresting cover art to reach out and grab a comic you'd normally pass by. This is an impulse you should learn to resist if you ever expect to stay within your buying abilities.

Many comic-book shops will be more than glad to "pull" a copy of each new issue on your buying plan, in order to assure that you'll never miss out on your favorites. Only after you've scanned the books that have been pulled for you and made those purchases according to plan should you indulge in window shopping for impact covers and impulse buys.

Remember, too, that a new comic will probably cost you more after it has moved into back-issue, or back-stock, status. Therefore, its original cover price is probably the best deal you'll ever get on it, so you should seriously consider buying the comic when

Fig. 3-1. *Nyoka* #4. Occasionally photographs are used on the covers of comics, but that is the exception, rather than the rule, since the art form is basically pen-and-ink illustration. (© Fawcett Publications)

Fig. 3-2. *True Crime* #1. Reprints of controversial stories from the past became a very popular staple of independent publishers in the 1970s. (© Eclipse Comics)

Fig. C-1. This *Alter Ego* #4 infinity cover seems to go on forever. Such covers provided popular collecting subcategories. (© First Publications)

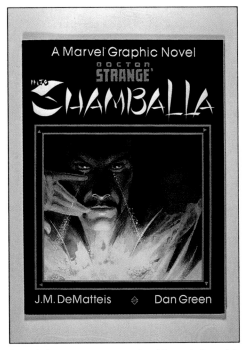

Fig. C-2. An example of a Marvel Graphic Novel. One of the first mature formats for contemporary comics. (© Marvel Entertainment Group)

Fig. C-3. *Creepy* #113. Horror stories were published in magazine format to avoid the Comics Code Authority. (© Warren Publications)

Fig. C-4. *Mighty Mouse Fun Club Magazine* created a spirit of friendship among comic readers. (© Terry Toons)

Fig. C-5. The character crossover is a popular device for expanding readership and the illusion of reality in a comic-book world. (© Marvel Entertainment Group)

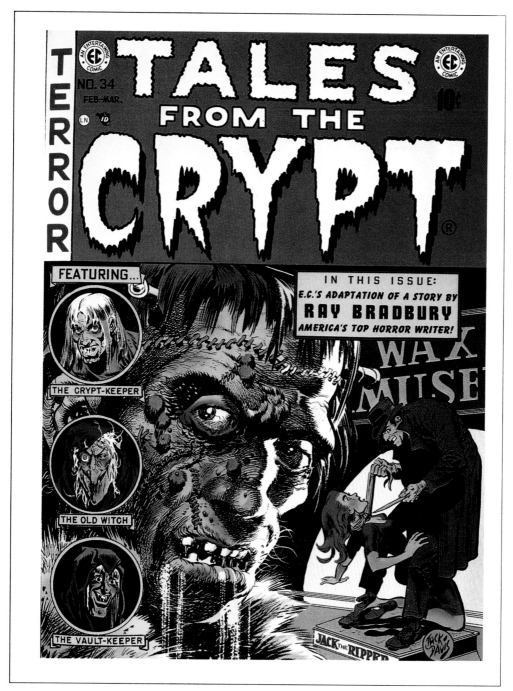

Fig. C-6. *Tales from the Crypt* #34. Typical E.C. horror comic that stimulated the establishment of the Comics Code Authority. (© E.C. Comics)

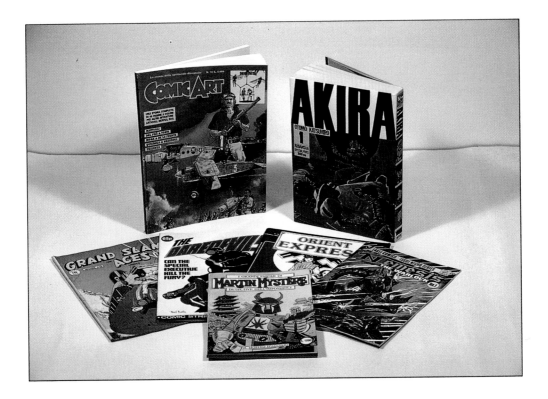

Fig. C-7. A selection of foreign comics.

Fig. C-8. This *Spirit* section published in the 1940s was a supplement to several Sunday newspapers. (© Will Eisner)

Fig. 3-3. *Zot* #2. Many of today's comics are related in content to other popular media forms, such as video games. (© Eclipse Comics)

Fig. 3-4. *The Punisher* #6. Today's comics tackle today's issues with macho style. (© Marvel Comics)

Fig. 3-5. *Doc Savage* #4. A second generation of Savage adventures drawn by a second generation of Kubert artists. (© DC Comics)

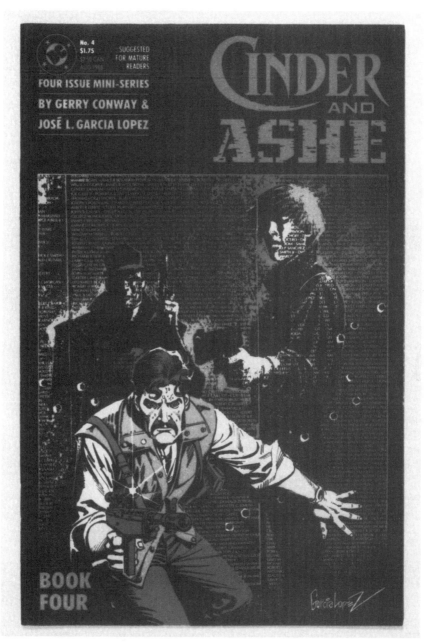

Fig. 3-6. *Cinder and Ashe #4*. Today's crime comics deal with hard, contemporary political and social issues. (© DC Comics)

Fig. 3-7. *American Flagg* #22. Many of today's science-fiction comics still rely on sex and violence. (© First Comics)

it first comes out, rather than waiting until later when the availability has gone down and the price has gone up.

A moment ago I mentioned *savings*. Why pay cover price for a new comic, when you can get it at a discount? Most comics shops will sell new comics to you at less than cover price. Why? Because to the comics shop where you're a regular your "pull" or buying list represents a sort of advance order; the shop can expect that you and everyone else who is a loyal customer will come in each week or month and buy the books that have been requested on the "pull" lists. This means that the shop can better estimate the correct size of its own order from the distributor warehouse and can operate more efficiently knowing what's likely to be requested in the future. In return for customer loyalty and support, most shops will return a percentage of a comic's cover price to regular customers who have an account. This discount can run as high as 20 to 25 percent, depending on the market conditions in a particular area.

Usually such a discount is offered only on new comics, but you should keep an eye out for any special deals offered by your shop on other items as well. One store in my area offers a once-a-month special in which one issue of a specific comic is sold at only a few cents over the store-owner's cost. This concept introduces customers to a title that is worthy of note but may not have been selling well lately, and it also increases the

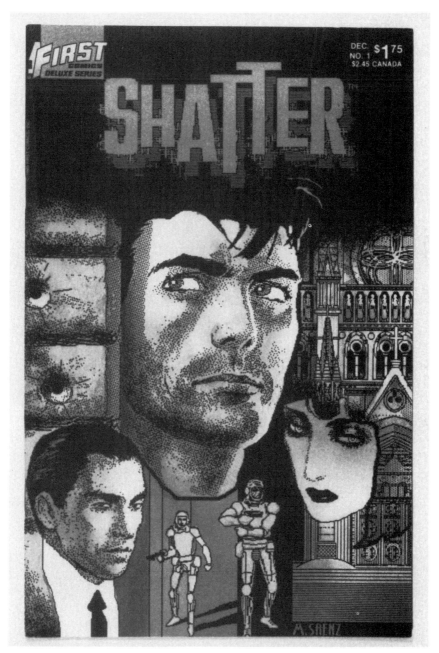

Fig. 3-8. *Shatter* #1. Unusual example of computer illustration techniques used in the creation of First Comic's *Shatter* series. (© First Comics)

Fig. 3-9. *Jonny Quest* #13. A popular animated TV series of the 1960s became a popular comic of the 1980s. (© Comico Comics)

Fig. 3-10. *G.I. Joe* #21. A popular animated TV series of the 1980s became a popular comics series at the same time. Some things never change. (© Marvel Comics)

comic's readership, at least for a while. Another shop has a twice-a-year 20-percent-off sale on all back issues. If you're patient, you can get many comics you need for less, once they go on sale.

Speaking of patience, there are even greater discounts available (some as high as 45 percent) if you can further control your urge to buy on impulse. All you have to do is order your comics by mail.

Several mail-order businesses offer a new-issue subscription service. Such a business buys hundreds of copies of every new issue and each month or every two weeks sends to its subscribers a list of the new comics available. If you are a subscriber and you receive the list, you check off the books you want and return the list with payment (money order or check so you'll have a record of the transaction) and the business sends you a box of all the new comics you ordered by mail.

Usually these independent subscription services charge a modest fee for postage and handling if your order is small, but many times there is no minimum order and you get your comics already bagged and in guaranteed Mint condition. Sometimes the postage will be paid by the service on moderate-sized orders, and free comics and promotional items are occasionally thrown in as well. All at a savings of up to 45 percent off!

Of course, there is one disadvantage to buying your new comics by mail: you do

Fig. 3-11. *The 'Nam #7*. Today's war comic is more realistic and less positive about military force. (© Marvel Comics)

Fig. 3-12. *Justice League International #1*. The Justice League of America went international in 1987. Some of its members have attitude problems—but just little ones. (© DC Comics)

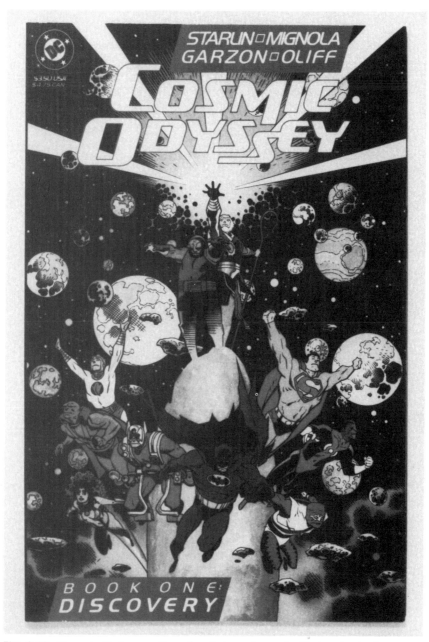

Fig. 3-13. *Cosmic Odyssey.* Premier deluxe format with laminated covers, 64 pages, and no ads gives today's comics their best exposure. Cover prices are at the level of most paperback books. (© DC Comics)

Fig. 3-14. *Millennium* #1. Today's miniseries with multiple crossovers to other books creates a sometimes-chaotic, sometimes-awesome media event. *Millennium* was perhaps the most entertaining and impressive story of 1987. (© DC Comics)

not get to see them before you buy them. But if you can be patient, you can save a bundle! Several of the subscription services advertise regularly in the comic-book news publications, and some even run ads in the actual comics. Check them out; they can provide some of the best deals around, especially if there isn't a comic-book shop in your area.

Finally, with all the new comics that come out each week, many collectors find that they don't have enough time to read everything they buy. If this happens to you, you should seriously think about getting some of your newer comics by trading with your friends. Perhaps the books that look only slightly interesting to you can be read and collected by swapping with other collectors. A comic can still seem new even when it's several months old, if you haven't read it. And there's little point in grabbing up all the new comics the day they appear, if you can't find the time to read them. So, talk it up. Keep in touch with other collectors, and you'll always have more ''new'' comics available to you than you possibly have time to read.

CHAPTER 4

The Best Way To Find and Buy Old Comics

IF YOU'VE EVER WANTED to be a detective, then tracking down old comics is a job you'll love. Twenty years ago it was easy to find old comic books from the 1940s and 1950s. All you had to do was put an ad in the local paper, and people would call you hoping to make a little extra cash by selling their "dumb old comics" to you.

It seemed that older folks (then in their forties) were always scanning the Sunday classifieds, and these were exactly the people who had old comics and wanted to sell them at a modest but reasonable profit. Usually, a dollar per comic seemed like a windfall profit to the individual who originally paid only a dime. Besides, if they couldn't sell them for just a little more than cover price, even if they were "used," they'd be just as happy to give the comics to their grandchildren. All this was before the advent of *The Official Overstreet Comic Book Price Guide* (hereafter noted as the *Price Guide*). In those old days, you would buy, sell, and trade comics at whatever rate seemed fair to both parties.

In the early 1970s, when the first edition of the *Price Guide* was published, some collectors complained that the prices were all wrong (usually "too low" if the collector was selling comics, and "too high" if the collector was buying). Other collectors didn't like the three-step pricing of Good/Fine/Mint because it didn't account for other common conditions, like Near Mint and Fair. Still other collectors found gaps, errors, and misprints throughout the guide.

Perhaps the most significant result of the publication of the *Price Guide* was that it "legitimized" comics in the minds of noncollectors and thus invited investors seeking a good profit into the hobby. However, many older collectors felt that this influx of investors caused comics prices to rise to the point where an average fan couldn't afford the treasures of the past, except in reprint.

In any event, controversies notwithstanding, the *Price Guide* continues to prevail,

Fig. 4-1. *Smash #79*. Jack Cole provides a humorous variation on Eisner's character Spirit with the creation of the character Midnight. Other characters in this series included Gramps and a talking monkey. (© Quality Publications)

mostly because the majority of collectors need some sort of reference tool with which to gauge the values of their collections. After all, money is important to everyone, and there's hardly a place left in the country that doesn't have awareness of and access to the *Price Guide*.

In the last two decades, tons of old comics have come out of the closets, attics, cellars, and, yes, even the woodwork (paper makes great insulation) to be graded, priced, bagged, and sold, until you'd think that every old comic ever saved or forgotten in storage has been rediscovered and resold at top prices. This is far from the truth. If it were, most antique and collectible shops would be out of business. Perhaps they know something you don't. Perhaps they are really good detectives who never give up until the quarry is tracked down. Even after you've finished reading this book and applied your skills to locating and acquiring old comics, there will still be thousands of books that you've missed and thousands more that can be bought at prices below those quoted in the *Price Guide*. Why? Because the *Price Guide* is only a *guide*—it is not the law. It's a starting point for negotiating a price, not an ending point.

But before you can negotiate the purchase of an old comic book you have to locate it, right? The rest of this chapter presents seven surefire ways to find old comics.

Fig. 4-2. *Boy* #42. Midnight was not the only character with a monkey assistant. Witness Crimebuster (C.B.), whose comic later became a variation on Lev Gleason's successful *Crime Does Not Pay* books. (© Lev Gleason Publications)

Fig. 4-3. *Jumbo #114.* Fiction House comics such as the one pictured used less-than-subtle artistic techniques to draw for the more "mature" male audience. (© Fiction House)

Friends, Relatives, and Countrymen

If you spread the word of your interest in comics throughout your family and neighborhood, you'll find that almost nobody thinks its a hobby to be ashamed of. These days, nearly everybody has read a comic book at least once in their lives, and it's likely that a lot of older comics are still lying around, just waiting to be read and collected by you.

Many people have heard that some old comics can be worth money, and this means two things. First, these people have decided not to throw their comics away, so the books are still available, if you ask for them. Second, you can buy these old comics without going through a middleman dealer, so the price should be very low. Of course, many of your older cousins, neighbors, and friends might *give* you their old comics when they find out that you collect. What's a few issues of *X-Men* or *Metal Men* between friends?

Local Ads and Fliers

Almost every neighborhood has a newspaper. There are local community papers, citywide daily and Sunday papers, "trading times," and campus newspapers. All of these have

Fig. 4-4. *Wings* #104. Comic books provided contemporary adventure themes for the young male audience, plus frequent use of the female form to enhance the pulse-pounding aspects of their content. (© Fiction House)

certain classified-ad categories, usually labeled "Collectibles" or just "Wanted to Buy," in which you can announce your interest in buying old comics. These ads often cost less than a couple of dollars (the price of a new comic?), and they are read by hundreds of people.

You'll need to list your telephone number, of course. And be prepared for calls at all hours. But an ad in a newspaper is an extremely effective way to spread the word in your community that you are hunting for old comics. I once got a call from the local television station because of a small ad I'd run in the evening paper. The reporters came out and produced an interview with me for the local evening news that kept my phone ringing for days.

Another way to get the word out involves using a graphics computer or a local quick-print shop to photocopy a stack of single-sheet fliers that you can distribute to flea markets, thrift shops, antiques stores, and even the local supermarket. This is also a good way to contact other collectors, who can be a source of back issues and a lot of good general discussion about comics.

Many dealers at thrift shops and antiques stores don't know what to do with the sort of items you're looking for. Their normal customers usually don't want to buy comics, so when the books turn up there's a good chance you can be the one to take them off a dealer's hands at a low, low price. Even if there are several comic-book stores in your area, be sure to check out all the rummage and garage sales you can. There are hidden treasures available every week during the spring-cleaning season.

Other Collectors

The time-honored method for assembling a collection of comics has always been to trade them with other collectors. Perhaps you can meet new collectors while visiting a comic-book shop or a convention. Perhaps you can pick up a few back issues while attending a meeting of your local comics club. By sharing your hobby with people who understand your interest, you can probably strike a good deal and swap lots of books while making new friends.

Auctions/Estate Sales

Many collectors find that the best way to buy lots of old comics is to scan the listings in the newspaper for auction notices and estate sales. Usually the itemized list of things to be sold will mention comics if they are available for sale, so these collectors just scan for the magic word. Then they attend the auction and bid on the books up for sale, just like an antique dealer bidding on Chippendale furniture.

In the last few years, even a number of the more prestigious auction houses in

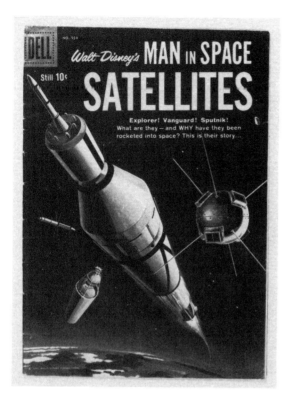

Fig. 4-5. *Man in Space.* The space age comes to comics by way of Walt Disney and Dell Publications. (© Walt Disney)

America have conducted day-long sales of comics and comics-related items. These auction houses include

- Christie's, 502 Park Ave., New York, NY 10022
- Lloyd Ralston Toys, 447 Stratfield Road, Fairfield, CT 06432
- Sotheby's, 1334 York Ave., New York, NY 10021

If you attend an auction, you may be required to pay a small fee for the privilege of placing a bid. But before the auction begins, you usually can look over the items up for sale. If the comics don't appeal to you, you obviously don't have to pay the fee because you won't be bidding. But if the books are ones you want to try to buy, get your identification number and hold on to your hat because this is where the fun begins.

Decide before you begin bidding how much you're willing to pay for the lot or lots of comics you've selected and inspect them carefully for any flaws or defects. It's easy, once the excitement of the auction begins, to get carried away and bid higher than you intended to. That's one of the reasons auctions go so fast. And once you've won the bid, there's no turning back: the comics are yours, lock, stock, and barrel.

Still, an auction is one of the most economical ways of acquiring old comics. There is usually not much competition; the items are there to be sold starting at rock-bottom

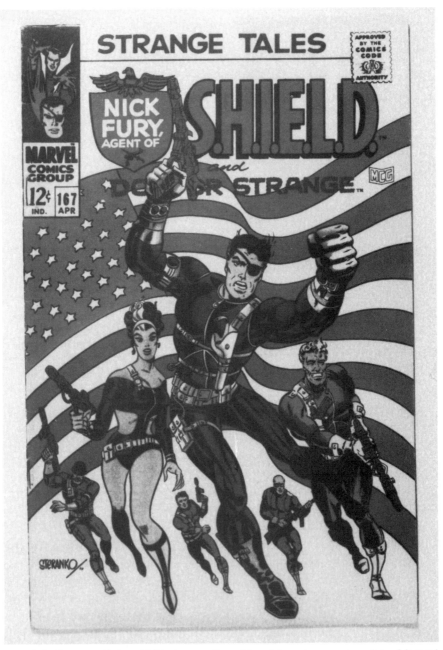

Fig. 4-6. *Strange Tales* #167. James Bond had to move over when Marvel Comics introduced *Nick Fury, Agent of S.H.I.E.L.D.* This issue features a four-page panel. (© Marvel Comics)

prices; and you have a good chance of coming away with lots of really old comics because the things being auctioned are often part of an elderly person's estate and are therefore quite old. Even if you are out-bid, don't dispair; you've still got your money for an auction listed in next week's newspaper.

Mail Order

As with new comics, as far as saving money is concerned one of the best ways to get *old* comics at good prices is to buy them by mail. Essentially, when you do this, it is the same as buying them from other collectors. The only differences are the distance and the fact that you do not get to see the comics before you buy them. This first point is not a problem, but the second point can be.

There are all sorts of ways you can buy comics by mail, and just about every old comic ever printed is for sale via mail order. So where and how do you find these mail-order dealers? Easy. Some are listed in the comic books themselves. Others can be found in ads in *The Comics Buyer's Guide* (hereafter referred to as the *Buyer's Guide*) and the *Price Guide*.

Here are the basics for buying by mail:

1. Compare prices. Try to inspect several lists at one time for the best deal.
2. Try to list some alternate choices in case the books you want are already sold. That way, you increase your chances of getting something for your efforts, instead of just your money back.
3. Place your order, paying by check or money order. Never send cash.
4. Be sure to enclose your name and address with your order, in case the envelope gets damaged or discarded.
5. Allow three or four weeks for your comics to arrive. If you haven't received a response in a month, write a polite note repeating your order information and asking when you can expect to receive your comics. If you hear nothing back after three more weeks, write a letter to the magazine where you saw the ad. After two more months, contact the post office to file a complaint. The post office may not be able to get your money back, but it can pursue fraud charges against improper use of the mails.

For protection, you might want to consider insuring your return package. When your comics arrive, inspect them carefully to be sure they are as advertised. Most dealers have a liberal return policy. If you're not satisfied, you can immediately return an item for a full refund. If you do return an item, make sure you insure it, and also send a letter to the dealer ahead of the package that explains why you are dissatisfied and are returning the comic.

An alternate method of buying through the mail is the mail-order auction. To participate in a mail-order auction you simply respond by a certain date to a listing in an ad

Fig. 4-7. *Boy Commandos* #15. Early continuing villain, who later fought Robin, the Boy Wonder. (© DC Comics)

or catalog with your best bid for a comic offered for sale. If you are the only bidder, you'll be notified that your bid has won and payment is due. If you are one of the top bidders, you may get a second chance to increase your bid. Some auction services provide a telephone number where you can call to see if yours is the leading bid, and, if it is not, you can rebid until the closing hour of the auction. This sounds complex, but it is very easy. A few calls can net you a premium book at a very low price.

Local Comic-Book Shops

Sooner or later, if you're patient, you'll find that everything goes on sale. Keep an eye on your local shop; these days most stores make their profits from selling new comics. Occasionally stores will offer incentives, like lower prices on older comics, just to keep the cash flowing. That's the best time to buy. When you decide to purchase a pile of old comics, ask the store if you can work out a discount for the whole pile. Granting you a discount isn't worth it to the store if you're only spending a little, but if you're buying in volume, it's customary to receive a break on the final total.

Comic Conventions

The volume discount technique works well at comic conventions, too. The really good deals are available near the end of a convention. If a dealer has made a lot of money, that dealer may feel comfortable about giving you a bargain. If a dealer hasn't made much money at all, that dealer might give you a discount in order to help cover his or her basic expenses. Some dealers actually enjoy haggling, trading, and bargaining. If you don't ask, you may never know what you've missed.

One final point about buying old comics at a convention, shop, or auction: Always treat the books with great care. Recall, if you will, that they are made of inexpensive paper that is probably decades old. If they are encased in plastic bags, don't take them out yourself. Ask the dealer to do that so you can fully inspect the comic. Hold the comic carefully, as you might a newborn baby—firmly enough that it can't fall out of your hands, but gently enough that you don't cause damage. Much of a comic's value depends on its condition. Never fold the pages back or lift the book by its cover. If you don't wish to buy the comic, hand it back and let the dealer handle the repackaging.

Condition is one of the most important aspects of collecting, and we will discuss it in greater detail later in this book. For now, just remember that while old comics are all around you and readily available from many sources, they are getting older and rarer every day. That's one of the reasons they're valuable.

CHAPTER 5

What Makes a Comic Valuable?

IN MY COLLECTION there are a number of comics I would easily sell if someone made me a quick and decent offer. These are comics I once thought I wanted or needed, but now feel I'll never read again. Also in my collection are many comics about which I feel lukewarm; these are books that I *might* want to read again someday, but I'm just not interested today, thank you. These are comics I might be willing to part with—or maybe not. If I let them go, I know I can always be able to get them back, because they're commonly available from several sources.

Finally, in my collection is a select group of books I would *never* part with. These are the heart and core of my collection, and I read and reread them every few years. Many other collectors agree that these are some of the greatest comics ever published, and these books are hard to find because lots of people like them.

To my way of thinking, the books in this latter group of "special" comics are the most valuable. They may not be the highest-priced books, but they would be the first ones I'd think of saving if my house were going up in flames. To me, they're priceless and cherished. To other people, they're only junk. But that's okay. I like 'em, and they're mine. And that's the best way to evaluate the worth of one comic over another.

Notwithstanding the above comment on personal taste, there are several objective traits common to the greatest treasures in most comics collections. The rest of this chapter focuses on the basic reasons why a comic book is considered valuable by a majority of collectors.

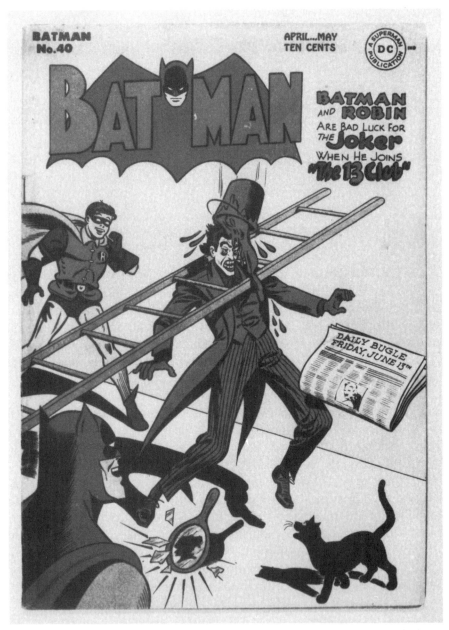

Fig. 5-1. *Batman* #40. Another example of Batman's most colorful villain (pun intended). (© DC Comics)

Fig. 5-2. *Detective Comics* #125. The ever-popular Batman and Robin faced not only a host of colorful villains but also more realistic crime-fighting dangers, such as the firing squad shown here. (© DC Comics)

Fig. 5-3. *World's Finest* #27. Robin, the Boy Wonder, was for many young readers the perfect entrée to the world of adult superheroes. Even after Robin's death in 1989, DC quickly saw the need to revive this important character. (© DC Comics)

Fig. 5-4. *Elfquest* #30. In a rare instance, the *Elfquest* series of Windy and Richard Pini was picked up for republication by Marvel Comics for a major redistribution to a larger audience. (© Marvel Comics)

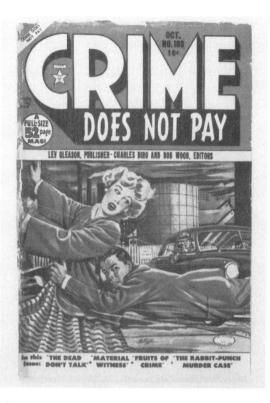

Fig. 5-5. *Crime Does Not Pay* #103. In an attempt to emulate the successful pulps, many comic books of the 1940s and 1950s had fully painted covers. (© Lev Gleason Co.)

Fig. 5-6. *Dr. Doom* #20. By the late 1960s, the Comics Code Authority had relaxed enough for Marvel Comics to produce a book featuring the villain, rather than the hero. (© Marvel Comics)

Fig. 5-7. *From Beyond the Unknown* #17. Presidential appearances in comics were always rare. This 1970s reprint version of a 1950s story covered the image of Eisenhower with the features of Nixon in order to keep the story contemporary. (© DC Comics)

Artistic Aspects

Someone referring to the "artistic aspects" of a comic may be speaking of the writing as well as the drawing, but this is not typically the case. The term *artistic* is primarily used to describe the style and quality of the person who illustrates the story. (Many times this is also the person who wrote the comic, too, so there's often no need for a distinction or for clarification.)

Throughout the years, there have been many important artists who have influenced the look of comics, major artists whom others have sought to imitate. These creative individuals can make a world of difference in the value of a comic by the contribution of their art. Consequently, many collectors specialize in books containing major artists like Jack Kirby, Frank Frazetta, Will Eisner, and Carl Barks. If you aren't familiar with these artists, you should try to learn all you can about them and to recognize their work.

Jack Kirby invented the patriotic hero comic (*Captain America*, 1941) the kid gang comic (*Newsboy Legion* and *Boy Commandos*, 1942), and the romance comic (*My Date*, 1947), just to name a few of this remarkable man's achievements. Frank Frazetta brought a realistic vitality to comic books in the early 1950s with a single issue of *Thunda* and a handful of E.C. stories. Will Eisner crafted the guidelines of sequential art in his weekly *Spirit* newspaper supplement and taught generations how to fill a mere "comic book" with character and depth. Carl Barks wrote and drew hundreds of Donald Duck stories, creating the charming and humorous Uncle Scrooge, who roamed the world for decades seeking wealth and adventure.

Kirby, Frazetta, Eisner, and Barks are just a few of the important contributors to the field of comic-book art. Here are a few more:

Artist	Classic Comic Work
Neal Adams	Deadman, Batman, Avengers
Matt Baker	"Good Girl Art"
John Byrne	Superman, X-Men, She Hulk
Jack Cole	Plastic Man
Johnny Craig	E.C. Crime and Horror
Reed Crandall	E.C. Horror and Humor
Jack Davis	E.C. Horror, Humor, and War
Steve Ditko	Spider-Man, Dr. Strange
Bill Elder	Mad, Panic
Lou Fine	Black Condor, The Ray
Graham Ingles	E.C. Horror
Walt Kelly	Pogo
Joe Kubert	Hawkman, Tor, Sgt. Rock
Harvey Kurtzman	Mad, Two-Fisted Tales
Moebius	Lt. Blueberry, Arzach
Bob Powell	Mr. Mystic, Red Hawk
Barry Smith	Conan, Machine Man

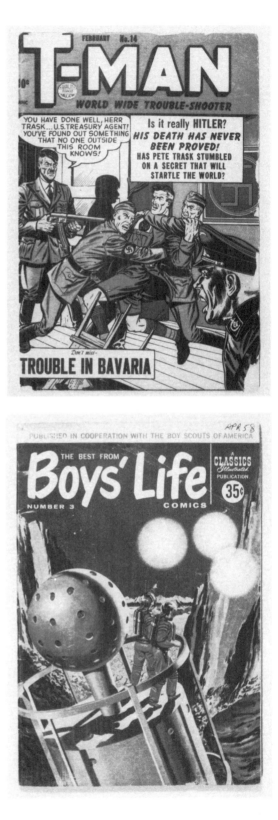

Fig. 5-8. *T-Man* #14. Adolph Hitler, a noted villain in both the comics and the real world, continued to hold sway over the comics as late as 1954. (© Quality Comics)

Fig. 5-9. *Boy's Life* #3. *Classics Illustrated* joined *Boy's Life* magazine in the late 1950s to create a series of comics reprints from the magazine's popular features. (© Gilbert Publications)

Jim Steranko	Nick Fury
Dave Stevens	Rocketeer
Alex Toth	Zorro, Bravo for Adventure
Al Williamson	E.C. Science Fiction
Basil Wolverton	Atlas Horror Comics
Berni Wrightson	Swamp Thing, Batman

This list may change with the whims and fancies of popular taste, but you'll find that any of these names on a comic will amost always mean a higher value. These artists are the "bankable stars" of the comic-book industry.

And don't forget the "Old Masters" from the newspaper strips: Hal Foster, Milton Caniff, Burne Hogarth, and Alex Raymond. People are still studying, copying, and collecting their work today. You can find them in many reprint comics that are themselves quite valuable.

Historic Importance

The first time something important happens is usually more historic than the second time. In movies, a sequel or a remake may be better than the original, but it didn't start a trend—it followed one. On television, it is usually the first episode that introduces the main characters and sets up the world they live in, not the second. However, this has not been the trend in current comics.

While the premiere issue of a comic is usually worth more than the issues which follow, this higher value is sometimes due to a low print run or the obscurity of a title, rather than to the first issue's establishment of a leading character. Many new comics don't reveal the "secret origin" of their characters until the sixth or seventh issue. In this way, the publishers create suspense and allow themselves the opportunity to incorporate feedback from the readers in order to better focus the book to its audience.

So which issue is the most valuable, the #1 issue or the origin issue? The answer is both: the #1 issue because it sets the trend and the origin issue because it answers the burning questions that have grown out of the suspense from earlier issues. Other historical events in the comic's story line can make a particular book more valuable than the issues that come before or after it. For example, a major character might die, change costume, or begin a long series of adventures centered on a significant change in the story (for example, a character might get pregnant, struggle with alcoholism, or be banished into outer space).

Other historical aspects of valuable comics include anniversary numbers like issue 50, 100, or 500. Sometimes the last issue of a comic is more valuable than other issues because, like the first issue, it signifies a key point in the span of a trend. Crossover and cameo appearances can also make a comic more valuable. Sometimes such appearances mark the beginning of a major trend, such as the first time Superman met Batman, or

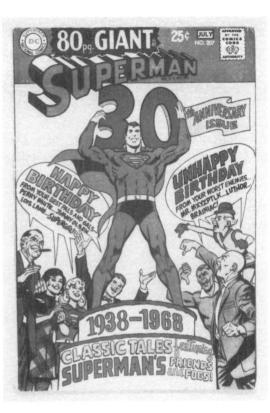

Fig. 5-10. *Superman 30th Anniversary Issue* #207. Superman, now over 50, took every occasion to celebrate his anniversary. (© DC Comics)

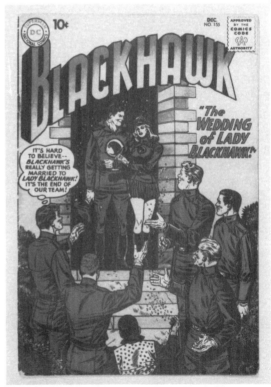

Fig. 5-11. *Blackhawk* #155. Marriage, always a topic of interest to adolescent males, was commonly only a hoax or a dream until the mid-1960s, which saw the wedding of DC's The Flash and Marvel's Fantastic Four. (© DC Comics)

Fig. 5-12. *Crossfire* #12. Cameo appearances by famous film stars always
spice up a comic's sales. (© Eclipse Comics)

Fig. 5-13. *Master of Kung Fu* #50. The interest in kung fu in the 1970s gave Marvel Comics an opportunity to bring back Fu Manchu from the 1920s. (© Marvel Comics)

Fig. 5-14. *Captain Carrot* #14. Superhero funny animals, a comics concept destined for success. Yet *Captain Carrot* lasted only a year and a half. (© DC Comics)

Fig. 5-15. *Crisis* #7. The death of Supergirl. Wagner would have been proud.
(© DC Comics)

the Hulk battled the Thing. Other times, there is a rare appearance of an actual person, such as the artist, the editor, or a famous rock star or boxer, within the confines of the story. It used to be something rather special if the President of the United States appeared in a comic, but lately that doesn't seem so unusual.

Lastly, a comic can be valuable because it contains subjects of historical significance. Incidents of strong sexual or drug-related content depicted in the newsstand comics of the 1950s are sought by historians, since it was this type of book that promoted the formation of the Comics Code Authority (see *Comics Code* in Glossary). Other subjects from this period, such as nuclear war, communism, and bondage, also draw higher interest—and, thus, lead to higher comics values.

Character Popularity

By far the easiest way to select and collect valuable comics is to pick a popular character to follow and collect. But watch out! Some recent comics characters have only been hot while their movie or television show has been playing, and even that's not always the best test for a popular character. Even before the recent Batman movie appeared at the theatres, there was a huge interest in old and new Batman comics. But the ''Superboy'' television series was not strong enough to boost the character back into comics until after the beginnning of the show's second season.

Don't assume that a lot of public exposure will always put a character into high demand right away, or a comic into the higher value brackets. With Golden Age comics, you're pretty safe in applying this logic, but with recent comics it's not always the case.

This point leads us to a discussion of forces *outside* of a comic's basic content and characteristics that affect its value, forces such as supply and demand and an individual book's condition.

Supply and Demand

Basic economics tells us that if the population's desire for an item increases while the number of that item available decreases, then the item's price will go up and continue to go up as long as the demand increases and the supply diminishes. In comics this means that the more collectors there are for, say, *Action #1*, and the fewer copies there are because of the effects of time, the higher the value of any one copy of *Action #1*.

In the last few pages we've discussed several factors that increase the demand for a specific comic—but what makes a certain one become rare or scarce? To begin with, comics, like most magazines and newspapers, are dated material printed and distributed for only a short time before the next issue is produced and the cycle continues. That's why comics need to be collected. Typically, they are not stored and filed at public libraries.

Fig. 5-16. *Justice League of America* #123. In a unique break from standard story lines, the villains of this comic are its writers. (© DC Comics)

Fig. 5-17. *All-Star Squadron* #37. Superman versus Captain Marvel. It was the battle everyone wanted to see, so DC Comics presented it at least four different times. (© DC Comics)

Fig. 5-18. *All-Star Squadron #23*. The black superhero, after many attempts, has yet to catch on in the world of comic books. (© DC Comics)

Fig. 5-19. *Cynicalman* #1. Minimalist comics.
(© Eclipse Comics)

Fig. 5-20. *Adventure* #267. An early appearance of the popular Legion of Super Heros.
(© DC Comics)

Fig. 5-21. *Daredevil Graphic Novel.* The fully painted panels of this book brought comics art up from its traditional pen-and-ink style. (© Marvel Comics)

Fig. 5-22. *Captain Midnight #52.* Like many other comic-book characters, Captain Midnight also appeared in movies and on radio and television during the 1940s and 1950s. (© Fawcett Publications)

Fig. 5-23. *Golden Lad #2.* Beautiful example of youthful superhero from the 1940s. (© Spark Publication)

Neither are they kept in print beyond their original publication date. So, when they're gone, they're gone. And that has a lot to do with why the older ones are so hard to find.

Then, too, many of the early issues of particular comics series have had very low print runs. This means that the publisher produced only a small quantity of books at the beginning of a series, waiting and hoping that the comic would be a hit. Later, after it was apparent that the comic was in great demand, the print run on succeeding issues was increased to meet the growing demand.

But the first time out, there's little information available to the publisher to help it guess the correct number of books to print. Nearly all comics publishers are not in the business of warehousing back issues. If you think about it, neither is your local newspaper. So the books produced in the original low print run are all that are available to be collected, unless the comics are reprinted—and that doesn't happen very often. Even when it does, a reprint is not considered to be as valuable as the history-making original.

In addition to all of this, comic books have been the victims of several generations of destruction. In the 1940s, they were bundled up for wartime paper drives. In the 1950s, they were publicly burned by people who thought that comics caused deliquency in minors. And in general, they have been paged through, stacked loosely in closets, scribbled on, and cut up by kids for over five decades. During this time, they've provided a lot of laughs and thrills, but all that wear and tear makes a comic book in good condition a relatively rare article.

Simply because a comic is old or rare, however, does not mean that it is valuable. If no one collects it and there is no demand, it doesn't matter what the supply is. Who cares? In the comic-book field, it is impossible to gauge supply, and demand is subjective and difficult to determine or predict. A comic is valuable when someone wants it. The more people who want it and the harder it is to get it, the higher is its value.

But what about two different copies of the same comic? Many times, one has a greater value than another. This difference in value hinges on condition.

Condition

Let me say right off that, unlike stamps and coins, a comic that is defective when it is produced is worth *less* than a normal copy. So when you're buying, be sure you select a copy that is evenly trimmed and is free of smudges and wrinkles and any sort of writing or fading on the cover. When you store your collection, be careful to protect it from excess heat, light, and moisture (see Chapter 8).

Two different copies of the same comic can have great difference in value simply because of the condition of the two copies. Desirable comics are comics that somehow seem to have just come off the stands, even if they're decades old. It's funny, but collectors want to imagine that they just bought every comic in their collection. It's a sort of trip back through time when they look at their books. And it's part of the charm of comics collecting. But a damaged book, even if it would otherwise be valuable, can bring only a fraction of its potential worth if it were undamaged.

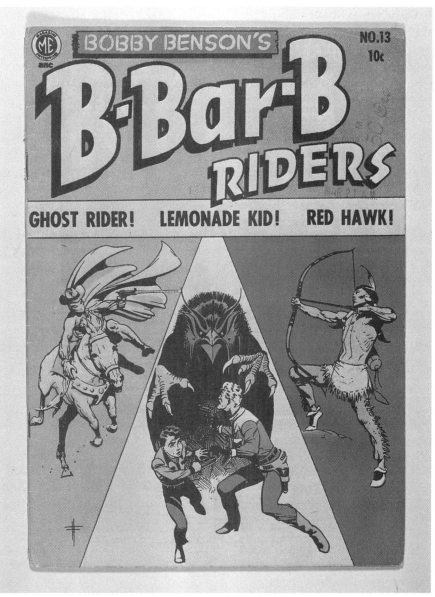

Fig. 5-24. *B-Bar-B Riders* #13 with Frazetta art and faded color cover. The art is wonderful, but the comic's condition is disappointing. (© Magazine Enterprises)

Traditionally, comics are separated into several grades of condition. You can do this by looking at a particular book and honestly describing what you see, which may be anything from an absolutely perfect copy to one that is extremely worn, dirty, and torn. Numerous variables influence the evaluation of a comic's condition, and all must be considered in the final grading decision. It is very important for a person grading a comic not to allow wishful thinking to influence what the eyes see.

It's tough to be objective when applying a grade to comics in your collection, especially if you're trying to sell them. But once you have found all of the defects in a comic, you will be ready to assign it a single grade. If you can't decide between two different grades, it's a good idea to assign the lowest one to be safe. The grades are listed and discussed in the next few paragraphs.

Mint (M): Comic book is in perfect condition in every way with no creases, nicks, tears, writing, or any other defects. Comic has white pages and a tight, bright, clean cover. Perfect. 'Nuff said.

Near Mint (NM): Very close to Mint. Comic is clean, flat, bright, and tight, and interior pages are white. No stress wrinkles along spine or wear along staples. May have a very minor defect or a date stamp. Near-perfect with no tears, creases, wrinkles, stains, or tape.

Very Fine (VF): A nice clean comic with only minor defects. A Very Fine comic is like a Near Mint comic except that the Very Fine comic will have slight wear near the staples, minor stress along the spine, or a tiny crease near the corner. Still no tears, stains, wrinkles, or tape.

Fine (F): A well-read comic that has developed obvious wear. Comic is still clean and flat, but there are some defects. A fine comic may have slight creases and stress wrinkles along the spine. There may be stress wear along the staples and minor creases near the corners.

Very Good (VG): Very Good describes the average comic. A Very Good comic is a heavily read comic. Comic may have several stress wrinkles, creases along the edges and corners, and stress wear. It will not have tears, stains, writing, tape, or missing pages.

Good (G): A Good comic is a very worn comic, and it may have many creases, wrinkles, and stress wear. A Good comic may also have minor stains, writing, and very minor tears, but no tape or missing pages.

Fair (FA): A Fair comic book is a worn and abused comic. It has multiple creases and wrinkles. It may also have stains, tape, writing, and tears. Nonetheless, a Fair comic is still complete.

Poor (P): An uncollectible comic. A Poor comic may have large tears, missing pages, and other heavy damage. It's usually no longer worth the paper it's printed on.

Coverless (C): Of special note are Coverless comics. If you have the body of the comic and are missing the cover, you might want to hang onto it until you find another damaged copy. Sometimes you can cleverly combine the best of the two copies and create something that will enhance your collection. This is also true for comics that have lost their center pages. Color photocopying can increase the value a little, too. Think of these recombined comics as Fair at best.

In addition to wear defects, there are a number of printing defects that can make a comic book less than desirable. For example, the cover may be miscut, the color may not line up perfectly, or the staples may not be centered on the spine.

If a book isn't Mint when you buy it, it never will be. But don't just assume that any *new* comic you buy is necessarily a Mint comic. It's possible that some shipping damage or handling wear may have occurred, or another prospective purchaser may have wrinkled or smudged the book while it was on the stands.

There are many complex details to consider when deciding on a value for your comics, among them historic aspects, artistic aspects, condition, content, and supply and demand. But don't let the apparent complexity of valuing comics bother you. With a little practice, you will quickly learn which comics have the highest value on today's market. At the same time, don't be surprised if someone still thinks that your priceless, invaluable collection is just a lot of junk. Everybody's tastes are different.

CHAPTER 6

Don't Get Burned

IMAGINE THE FOLLOWING SCENARIO (unless you don't need to imagine it because it has already happened to you):

You've just bought an old issue of your favorite comic. You're excited and can't wait to get home to pore over it. You rush in the door, set the comic down, and begin to read, only to discover that the centerfold is missing! Or the inside pages of the comic are different from the cover. Or someone has used the comic to cut out pictures for a scrapbook.

Does this kind of aggravation sound familiar? Such experiences are frustrating and disappointing, and they point out two important rules about collecting comics. *One:* Don't get so excited about buying, selling, or trading your books that you lose your common sense and make a terrible mistake. Be careful. Take your time and get excited later when you're reading the comic, not when you're buying it. *Two:* Look before you buy. Many perfectly good deals can literally turn to dust in your hands if you don't inspect the merchandise before you buy it.

Now that you have an understanding of the grading system discussed in the last chapter and can see how condition affects the value of your comics, it is important for you to learn how to spot specific defects within a comic that cause the book to be graded Good, when at first glance it seems to be in Mint condition. In other words, you need to learn how to "buy smart."

There are three major types of imperfections in comics that lower their value. These flaws result from *aging, wear,* and *printing.*

Aging Flaws

Like everything else, comics deteriorate as they grow older. It's natural and expected. You might think that it's perfectly acceptable to find a 40-year-old comic with yellow and brittle pages and rusty staples due to the normal effects of time. It might seem as if this condition is so normal that the comic should earn the grade of Mint just for having survived all those years.

If this sounds reasonable to you, you need to rethink the situation, because most collectors would not agree. After all, would you want a yellow, brittle comic in your collection if you could have the same book with smooth, white, and strong pages? It's possible to obtain such a nice, clean copy, if the book has been stored properly during its lifetime. I'll tell you more about storage and preservation in the next chapter, but for right now let's agree that the normal effects of time on a comic can be held at bay, if you know what you're doing. The grade placed on a comic is a description of the book's *condition,* not its *age.* Mint always means Mint, no matter what year the comic was produced.

Wear Flaws

Wear flaws are the most common defects suffered by comics. They occur when a comic is read, handled, and mishandled.

Worn or rolled spine: Just reading a comic will put wear on the spine. Laying the book flat and creasing the spine does even more damage. If you fold back the cover and the pages as you read a comic, you ''roll'' the spine, which is the worst damage you can do to a book's spine short of ripping it apart. In fact, rolling the spine usually causes so much stress on the comic that the cover can break free from the pages at the staples.

Cover wear: During normal reading, the outer cover of a comic will usually suffer some damage. Remember, you handle the cover every time you turn a page, assuming that you hold the book at all. It is better to set the comic down on a clean dry surface when you read it. This means you only touch the cover once or twice, and there is less chance of denting, smudging, wrinkling, creasing, or nicking it. The combined effects of normal usage will make your comic less than perfect. Be careful to keep these effects to a minimum.

Writing: Some collectors will ignore a vendor's arrival date stamped or written on a comic's cover, while others will not. This date is the only acceptable form of writing that can appear on a comic. Scribbling and the filling out of coupons in ads will detract from a comic's value and grade. Usually even an autographed comic is considered to be a flawed comic. Comics are not coloring books; they were made for reading, not writing.

Cuts, tears, and creases: Cuts, tears, and creases are perhaps the most noticeable forms of damage a comic can suffer. Coupons may be clipped, and covers may be wrinkled and loose. Heavy wrinkles and creases lower the value of a comic in the eyes of a collector, even if the comic has not been cut or torn.

Fig. 6-1. *Superman* #149, a comic that has given lots of pleasure to its careless reader, resulting in wear and a rolled spine. (© DC Comics)

Tape: Collectors who don't know any better often use tape to repair a comic. But tape can age, too. It often soils the comic with chemical oils and can, over time, do more damage than it appears to correct. *Never* be tempted to apply tape to your comics.

Water damage and stains: Tape is only one of the sources for the soiling of a comic. Others include food, mildew, and high humidity. These flaws cannot be corrected, but they can be avoided with care and proper storage conditions.

Critters: Insects and rodents can infest a comic and chew away its value. You've heard of bookworms, of course, and many other critters love to feast on the tender pages of comic books. Don't let this sort of disgusting thing happen to your collection.

Missing pages: Count the pages of any old comic you buy and be certain the complete book is there. After awhile, you'll find you can almost tell if a page is missing simply by the feel of the book. Each story should be complete. It's easy to forget that a comic in your collection has a page out, and it's embarrassing when someone else (a potential buyer?) points it out.

Printing Flaws

As mass-produced products, comic books can reach the stands with minor defects in individual issues. We mentioned this in the last chapter. It's important to remind you to be very selective when buying both new and old comics for your collection. A book with its staples off-center or its printing off-register is a less-than-perfect, less-than-Mint book, even when it's brand-new. A double cover or a missing staple is a rarity and an oddity. Most collectors prefer to own a complete and well-made copy over a misprint.

Abbreviations That Describe Flaws

Since comics are so vulnerable to flaws and collectors are so concerned about identifying these flaws, a standard series of abbreviations has developed over the years to quickly describe and classify a comic's imperfections during storage or sales. Here are most of the commonly used defect abbreviations:

BC:	Back cover
BR:	Brown or brittle
C:	Coverless
CC:	Coupon clipped
CF:	Centerfold (the center pages of a comic)
CFL:	Centerfold loose
CFO:	Centerfold out (the center pages are missing)
CHP:	Chip (small piece missing)

Fig. 6-2. False cover. A reproduction or photocopy cover of *Action* #52 has been added to this coverless comic. (© DC Comics)

CL:	Cover loose
CR:	Crease, or cover
NBC:	No back cover
PY:	Pages yellow
RB:	Rat-bitten
RRB:	Really rat-bitten
RS:	Rolled spine
SC:	Subscription crease (comic has been folded in half vertically by the publisher to be sent through the mail)
T:	Tape
TS:	Tape on spine
TP:	Tape repair
TR:	Tear
W:	Writing
WD:	Water damage
WS:	Water stain
WOC:	Writing on cover
Y:	Yellowing

This is not an official or complete listing. Common usage and creative combinations can provide for other descriptive phrases. A recent ad read, "Batman #34, rs, nbc, 2 in. tr on rfc, slight yel," which meant that the comic had a rolled spine, no back cover, a 2″ tear on the right front cover, and slight yellowing of its pages. Obviously, this was a very poor copy, but what the hey, if the price is right you just might want to buy it, and I'm sure you'd appreciate knowing about all the defects before you spend your money.

The good news in all this is that most of these defects can be avoided. You can actively keep them from occurring while reading and collecting comics, and you can avoid inheriting them by being extra careful when buying a new or "used" book.

Grading Comics

You should practice grading comics when you first begin collecting so you don't get too many chances to learn from big mistakes (that is, to get burned!). To help you get a handle on this tricky and somewhat subjective operation, I've provided a visual grading test for you and outlined the critical concerns for each grading category. The test consists of the color photographs in the insert following page 112 (Figs. GT-1 through GT-12), with answers at the end of this book, on page 215. Here are the critical concerns you should keep in mind while you take the test:

■ *Poor* comic has at least one of the following: *brittleness, torn or heavily soiled pages, a loose cover, ink scribbling.*

Fig. 6-3. *Detective #177*. Looks Mint, but it isn't. See photos in "Defect-Spotter's Guide" for explanation. (© DC Comics)

Fig. 6-4. *Tom Mix Commandos Comics* were not sold in stores. This "give-a-way" comic was mailed as a premium to members of the Straight Shooters club. This copy shows extreme tape damage.

- A *Fair* comic has none of the above defects, but at least one of the following: *rusted or broken staples, many folds, creases or wrinkles, dark-brown pages, a chunk out of the edge or cover.*
- A *Good* comic has none of the above defects, but at least one of the following: *water stains, loose pages, tape, a split spine, small pieces out of the cover, light-brown pages.*
- A *Very Good* comic has none of the above defects, but at least one of the following: *dull, faded cover; slight tears; rolled spine; subscription crease; yellowed edges; light pencil marks.*
- A *Fine* comic has none of the above defects, but at least one of the following: *light creases, off-white pages, mild spine wear.*
- A *Near Mint* comic has none of the above defects, but at least one of the following: *small flecks of color missing at the edges of the cover, faint creases near the staples.*
- A *Mint* comic has none of the above, nor any other defects, *period.*

A study of the ''Defect-Spotter's Guide'' which follows this chapter will also help prepare you for the grading test. The rewards are high for collectors who learn how to grade comics properly and for those who can control their desire to possess a book without first carefully inspecting it. The best way to avoid getting burned is to *buy smart.* You get a nicer-looking collection and a greater value for the time and money you've invested, and you're a better businessperson, too.

You can't lose—if you're careful.

DEFECT SPOTTER'S GUIDE

GRADING TEST

Carefully inspect the comics in the next dozen photos and try to determine the proper grade for each. "Solutions to Grading Test" appear near the end of the book, preceding the index.

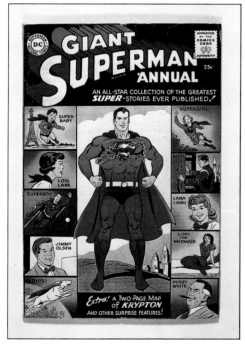

Fig. GT-1. *Superman Annual #1.* (© DC Comics)

Fig. GT-2. *Famous Funnies #179.* (© Eastern Color Printing)

Fig. GT-3. *Superman* #60. (© DC Comics)

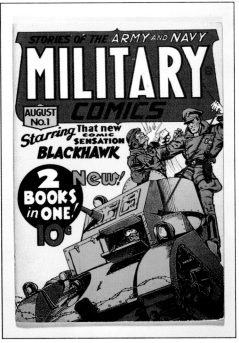

Fig. GT-4. *Military* #1. (© Quality Publications)

Fig. GT-5. *Big Shot* #77. (© Columbia Comics Group)

Fig. GT-6. *Doll Man* #14. (© Quality Publications)

Fig. GT-7. *All-Star Comics* #25. (© DC Comics)

Fig. GT-8. *World's Finest* #23. (© DC Comics)

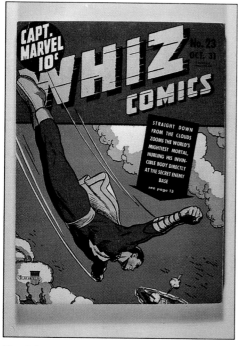

Fig. GT-9. *Whiz Comics* #23. (© Fawcett Publications)

Fig. GT-10. *Batman* #34. (© DC Comics)

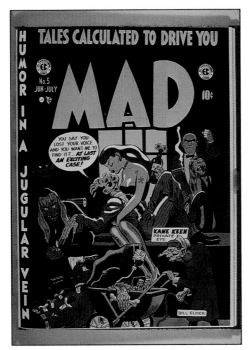

Fig. GT-11. *Mad* #5. (© E.C. Comics)

Fig. GT-12. *Action* #38. (© DC Comics)

Multiple creases. (© Fawcett Publications)

Ballpoint pen tracing on cover. (© DC Comics)

Ragged spine. (© Fiction House)

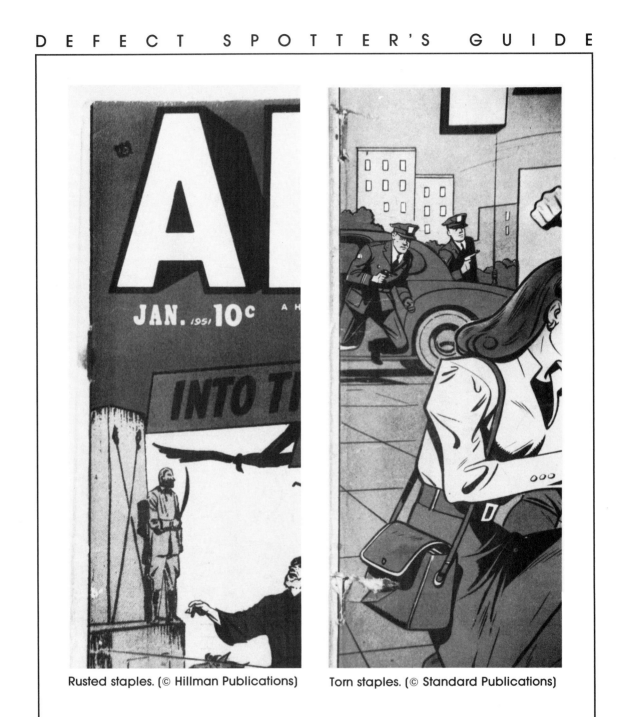

Rusted staples. (© Hillman Publications)

Torn staples. (© Standard Publications)

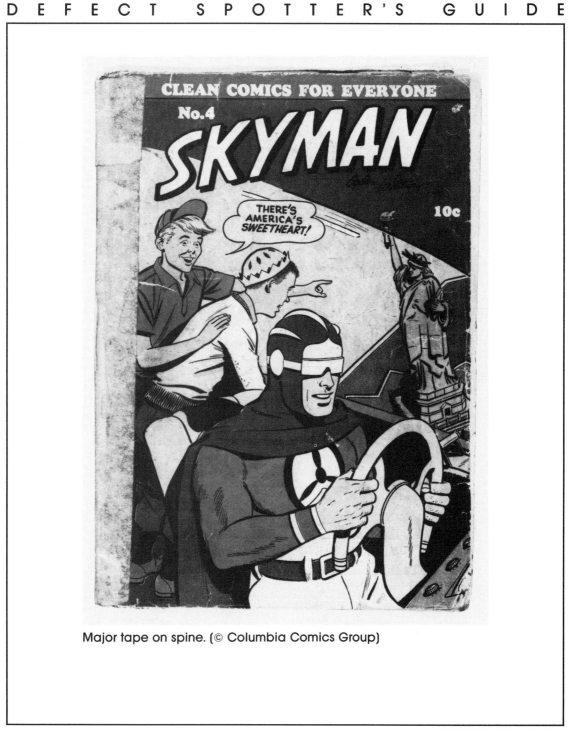

Major tape on spine. (© Columbia Comics Group)

Water spots. (© American Comics Group)

Date stamp and soiled cover. (© DC Comics)

Two-ring-binder holes punched in left side. (© Marvel Entertainment Group)

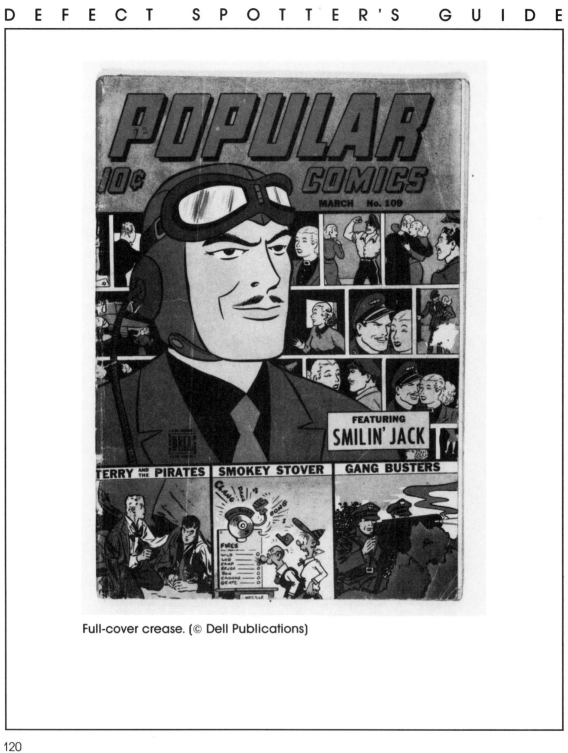

Full-cover crease. (© Dell Publications)

Major tape stain. (© Harvey Publications)

Slight tear in lower left corner. (© Eastern Color Printing)

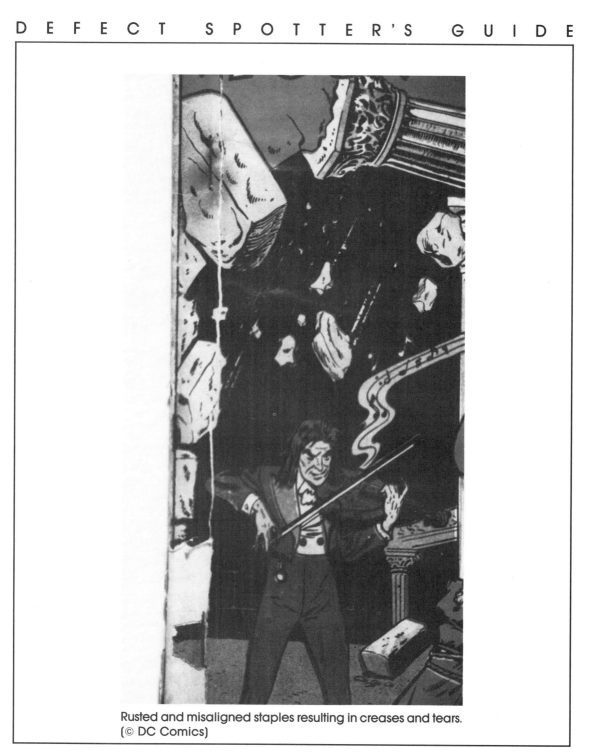

Rusted and misaligned staples resulting in creases and tears.
(© DC Comics)

Even *erased* pencil marks detract from a comic's value. (© Fawcett Publications)

Insect- or rat-bitten. (© Standard Publications)

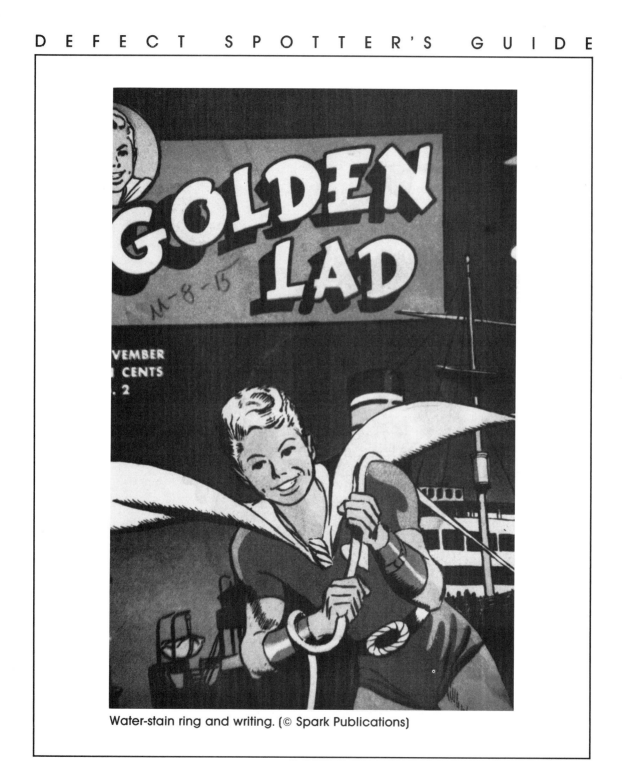

Water-stain ring and writing. (© Spark Publications)

Magazine retailer's date stamp. (© DC Comics)

Writing on cover. (© Dell Publications)

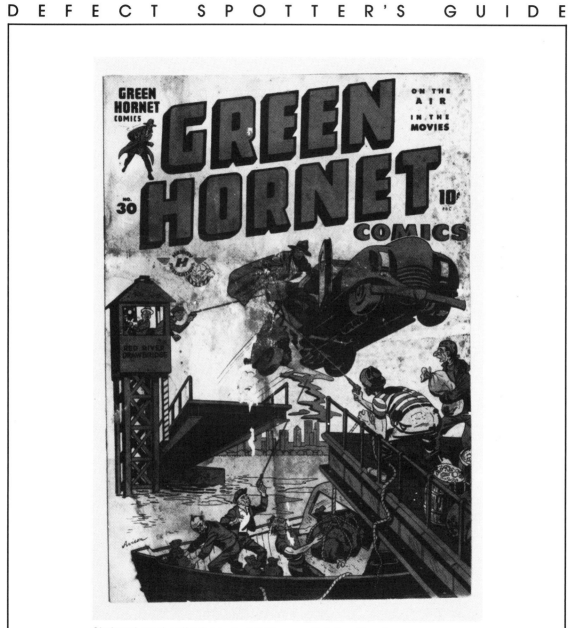

Stained and soiled cover. (© Harvey Publications)

Writing, and chips out of cover. (© DC Comics)

Slight cover wear and rolled spine. (© Marvel Entertainment Group)

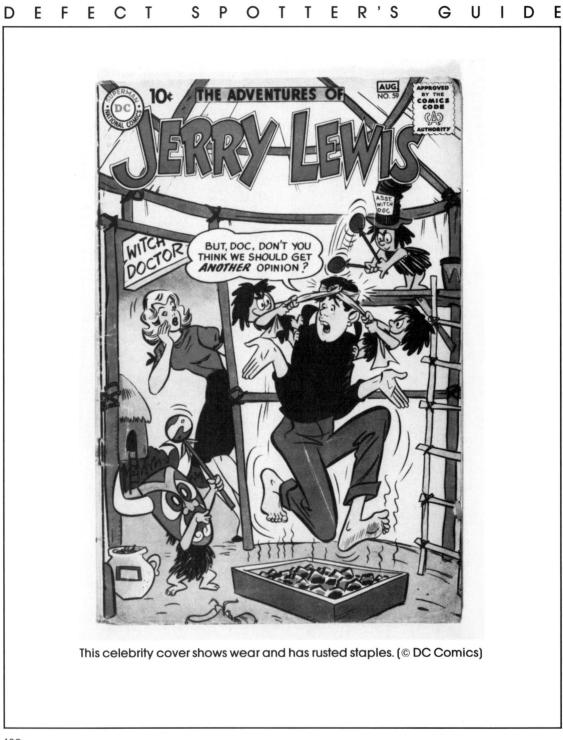

This celebrity cover shows wear and has rusted staples. (© DC Comics)

Water stains and heavy wear. (© DC Comics)

Subscription crease; tape and stitched spine (good intentions resulting in disaster). (© Harvey Publications)

Clipped coupon and rolled spine. (© DC Comics)

Oddly trimmed upper edge (look closely). (© DC Comics)

Telltale curve of paper on upper right edge indicates that comic had been trimmed in a paper cutter. When compared with another comic of the same era, this book is an eighth of an inch shorter. (© DC Comics)

This cover shows six fingers on Lois Lane's right hand. An artist's error that appears on all covers of an issue is not considered to be a defect and does not make an issue rare. (© DC Comics)

CHAPTER 7

The Comic Convention

REMEMBER CLEARLY my first comic convention. It was in New York City during the summer of 1972. I had read about these events in the comics publications, and I decided to make arrangements to travel to New York City and stay at the hotel where the convention was taking place.

As I registered and carried my bags to my room, I saw a familiar sight. Clustered around the lobby and on the elevators were small groups of collectors talking excitedly and holding stacks of rare and colorful comic books. Comics I'd never before laid eyes on! I could almost smell the old newsprint paper and four-color inks.

Minutes later, following the signs posted in the hallways, I arrived at a set of big double doors. There I paid a few dollars for admittance and then, for the first time, I stepped into the dealers room.

Here was a mecca, a bazaar, an enormous marketplace for old and new comic books. Thousands and thousands of books piled high or in boxes on a hundred dealers' tables. Comics of every size and description, condition and price. Immediately, I felt as if every comic ever published had to be somewhere in this room. As it turned out, I wasn't far from wrong.

I pulled my eyes away from the tables covered with comics and scanned the type-written schedule that I'd received while paying my admittance. There was a discussion panel of DC writers in gear at that moment in the hotel's main ballroom, but I never heard them. Nor did I hear any other panels that day. For the next dozen hours, I was busy—literally up to my ears in old and rare comics. Thank goodness I had thought to bring my want list, or I'd never have decided which comics to buy!

I soon discovered several dealers who were willing to consolidate the individual purchase of their books, so I was able to buy $20 of comics for less than $15. Part of the fun of the convention, I learned, was bargain-hunting and wheeling-and-dealing.

Hm-m, I thought. This is even better than I'd imagined. I bought a $5 comic for $4 and then sold it to another dealer for $6. Hm-m-mm! That's 50 percent profit! I bought three $1 comics and sold two of them for $1.50 each. That meant, of course, that the third comic was mine for free! *Hm-mm!*

But swapping and selling isn't the only thing you can do at a comic convention, because this is the place where it all comes together, all the hours of making lists, checking condition, tracking down valuable Golden Age goodies, and buying new comics the smart way. All the time, effort, and money invested in your favorite pastime pays you back in one big weekend of excitement: the comic convention.

Comic conventions are the big time, a collector's dream-come-true, where you get to do everything you've been doing at about 10 times the pace. You can meet other collectors, and you can talk to professional artists, writers, and editors to learn what's going to happen to your favorite character in upcoming issues. You can attend auctions, collect autographs, and sit in on panels that discuss important topics concerning comics. And you can buy, sell, and trade for as long as your money and your energy holds out.

The best way to find out about a convention in your area is to check for notices posted at your local comics shop. You can also scan the ads in publications like *The Comics Buyer's Guide* for listings in your area. Each year, there are hundreds of local, one-day conventions at hotels and shopping malls. Major cities host weekend conventions at least once each year. And a few monster comic conventions take place annually in cities like San Diego, New York, Chicago, Atlanta, Dallas, and Los Angeles. These are huge affairs that can threaten to sweep you away.

How to be a Smart Customer

After about 10 hours in the dealers room of my first convention, I was surprised to discover that my stomach was growling. I was starving for food. That reminds me of a good tip to pass on: *Never spend all of your money on comics*. Be sure you have enough set aside to cover the cost of your room, meals, and transportation. A friend of mine once had to sell back a number of comics at a loss to a dealer at the end of a convention because my friend needed cash to buy gas and food on his way back home.

Another tip: One of the best things you can do at a comic convention is wait. When you first arrive at the convention, pause before you buy anything. Take your time to carefully inspect the books you're eager to buy. Ask the dealer to hold them for you (for no longer than an hour); usually this arrangement is no problem, and it lets you test yourself and see if you really want to buy the books. It also gives you time to check out the offerings of the other dealers; you might find another copy of the same comic, but at a lower price.

There are other advantages to waiting while you're attending a comic convention. You should wait before deciding to buy any item, simply because it gains you the only power you have as a buyer other than the power of money: *time*. Time is to your advantage because there are so many opportunities to purchase comics at a convention that it's

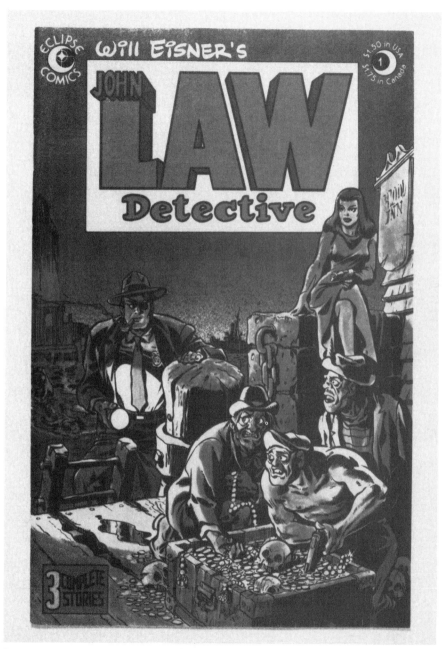

Fig. 7-1. *John Law Detective* #1. Some comics take decades to be produced. *John Law* was originally designed by Will Eisner in the 1940s, but did not see full publication until the 1980s. (© Will Eisner)

Fig. 7-2. *Spy-Hunters* #10. Even before the advent of the popular James Bond, the comic book heavily featured spies and spying. (© ACG Comics)

Fig. 7-3. *Shazam* #14. Due to a lapse of copyright, DC Comics found that it owned the rights to the Captain Marvel character, but not the use of his name in the title of the DC comic, since Marvel Comics had registered the name for its own use. (© DC Comics)

Fig. 7-4. *Jimmy Olsen #56*. DC Comic's popular "Imaginary Story" series let readers fantasize about the futures of their favorite heroes without affecting established story-line continuity. These tales "may or may not" someday happen, but I wouldn't bet on it. (© DC Comics)

somewhat a buyer's market. You might work up a deal with vendor #1 and put it on hold to work up a different deal with vendor #2. Perhaps then you can even go back to #1 and get an extra comic that #2 needs, thus improving your chances for a good deal with #2.

Another reason to wait is that many dealers don't want to pack everything up at the end of the convention and lug all their comics home. To avoid this chore, they will have a "going out of business" sale. On the last day of a convention, you can usually find several dealers who are willing to sell their comics at rock-bottom prices. When this happens, you'll be glad you held back some of your money to wait for these bargains.

When you conclude any deal and get ready to leave a dealer's table, pause for a minute. Double-check to be sure you have everything you should: the books you just bought, any other items you were holding (including your wallet), and the correct change. All the excitement of a comic convention will often distract you from these important things, and it'll be almost impossible to go back even after a few minutes to try to find or explain what you've lost or forgotten. There's no reward for buying fast. Take your time and do things right.

Here are a few more tips that will improve your experiences at a comic convention:

■ *Before you go to a convention, get that want list polished.* Believe me, when you're there, you'll see hundreds of tempting buys. There will be so many tantalizing comics

Fig. 7-5. *Humbug* #11. To compete with *Mad* magazine, other adult comics were created. *Humbug* magazine was distinctive because it used many of the old *Mad* artists and writers. (© Humbug Publishing)

that you'll soon lose track of what you need unless you can refer to your predetermined list.

- *Get there early*. If you wait until the second day of the convention, many of the choice deals will already have been snapped up. You want to be there when the doors open so you can inspect the best copies of your favorite comics and seek out the best prices. Remember, the greater the selection, the better your chances of finding the books you need. So get there early when the selection is the greatest.

- *Never buy a comic at the dealer's first price*. A comic convention is not a supermarket where everything is priced or marked down. If you want a discount, you will have to ask for it. Consider inspecting the grade and condition of a comic out loud. Sometimes the dealer will volunteer a lower price if you just inquire about a comic's condition.

- *Never leave your comics sitting out where dealers or other attendees can mistake them for their own*. It's a good idea to come to the convention with a carrying case of some sort that contains your name and address so you can easily reclaim your materials if they are lost.

- *Never be tempted to steal*. A comic convention may look like a lot of chaos, but it is not. Dealers know their wares, and they know how to protect them. No comic is worth the shame and embarrassment you'll suffer if you try to rip someone off. You expect to get a fair deal, and you should expect to give one, too.

- *Meet as many professionals as you can*. These people are there to give you an insight into the creative side of the comics business. You can learn a lot about what it's like to produce a comic, if you politely ask questions. You'll be amazed to find that most of the professionals are themselves collectors just like you.

- *At the end of the convention, take stock of the books you've purchased*. Inspect them a second time and try to recall which dealer or collector you got them from. If you discover any defects, hold on to the original bag, tag, and wrappings to prove that the book came from a specific dealer. Usually, you'll have no trouble returning the book at the next convention, assuming that there is a genuine problem with it. Convention dealers are just as conscious of good image as are the owners of your local comic-book shop.

How to be a Smart Dealer

After a few conventions, you might get the idea to set up a table yourself. No problem. It's easy to know in advance when a convention is scheduled in your area. Check the schedule listings in *The Comics Buyer's Guide* and look for listings of the rate for renting a table. This rental fee (from $20 to $150 per table, depending on the size of the expected convention attendance) will often include your admission to the convention, too.

Working a table can be a lot of fun, but it is also just what you might think: *work*. To begin with, you must have your books organized so that customers can easily find

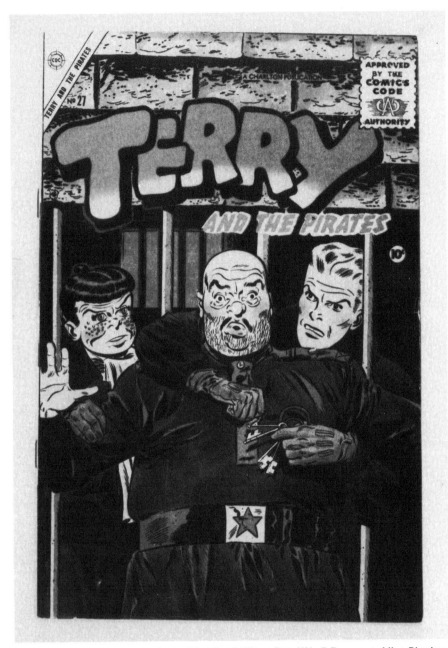

Fig. 7-6. *Terry and the Pirates #27*. After Milton Caniff left *Terry and the Pirates*, the strip was continued by George Wunder. After Harvey Comics left *Terry and the Pirates*, the comic was continued by Charlton Comics. (© Charlton Comics)

Fig. 7-7. *Daredevil* #182. Sometimes even the most fearless heroes have trouble dealing with the death of a loved one. (© Marvel Comics)

Fig. 7-8. *Boy Commandos* #2. Kids at war—what a concept. (This comic is in poor condition.) (© DC Comics)

what they're searching for. To protect the condition of your comics, you'll need a set of boxes to display your books and individual bags and backing boards to keep them in tip-top shape. And you'll have to lug them all into the convention hall early in the morning so you'll be set up and ready for business when the doors open.

You can expect to be asked a lot of questions about the comics you have for sale. Customers will want to know where things are and if you have a certain issue of a specific book. This means you'll need to know just what it is you're selling. And, of course, you'll need to make the correct change, to keep an eye on all your wares, and to try to work several deals at once with the droves of customers who want to buy your comics.

You are free to discount your comics as much as you like, whenever you like. Also, you might find that another dealer will be interested in buying up all the comics you have left at the end of the convention, if you offer a good bargain. One of the advantages of selling your leftovers this way is that you don't have to bother to pack things up when the convention is over.

The very best advice for being a dealer is the same as for being a customer: *Take your time*. Don't panic or allow yourself to be stampeded by the demands of the attendees. *Enjoy* yourself—it'll all be over before you know it.

CHAPTER 8

The Care and Feeding
of Your Collection

"**H**ERE," I SAID, "take my copy of the new *Superman* comic and read it." It was 1956, and I was doing what my mom always told me to do: I was sharing.

A couple of the neighborhood kids and I had decided to form a comic-book club. We'd pooled our collections and created a sort of lending library of comics. Now, Gary Hoffman, another kid from two streets over, wanted to join the club. So we gave him "The Big Test."

Gary stood there in his tattered sneakers and coonskin cap, eagerly yet suspiciously accepting the comic I'd offered. "What do you mean?" he asked. "Are you guys just going to watch while I read it?"

"Yeah," we answered, and Gary worried on that for a few seconds before scanning the comic's cover. We watched him like a hawk, man. Slowly, Gary opened the book. Then he read the first page. Then he turned the page. Then he folded back the cover and the first page and held the comic so he could study one page at a time. That's when we knew he didn't measure up.

"Whoa," we shouted. "Hold it right there, buddy."

I took back the treasured comic. "You're not reading *my* comics if you bend the pages back like that. You'll tear out the staples, dummy."

Too bad, Gary. You just didn't have a collector's instincts. You wanted to read the comics, but you didn't know how to keep them in good shape so you could reread them without having them fall to pieces.

"The Big Test" may seem a bit cruel, but it was a defensive measure learned the hard way. All too often I would loan out my prized comics, only to be disappointed by the battered returns. Most people are like Gary. They only want to *read* the comics, not collect them. Most people don't care enough to protect the books while they read them. They set a perspiring cola can on them, or eat a juicy sandwich over them, or smudge the cover with sweaty, greasy fingerprints. Or, they fold the pages back and put stress on the seams and staples. After all, it's only a comic. And in the 1950s, a comic only cost a dime. Right?

Not to a collector.

To a collector, comics are once-in-a-lifetime samples of delightful stories and entertaining art. Comics are doorways into other worlds of westerns, detectives, war, and outer space. Comics are superheroes and 'toons. Comics are something to be respected and cared for. Their fragile nature makes collecting them akin to butterfly collecting. It's a big and delicate job. Fortunately, there's help.

Handling Comics

To begin with, it's important to learn the proper method of handling comics. When you purchase a Mint-condition comic, it is best to read it once and file it away. Continued handling and reading will lower the condition no matter how careful you are, so if you plan on reading your comics more than once, you should purchase an extra copy for that purpose.

Here's how to properly handle a comic book that has already been inserted in a protective plastic bag:

1. When removing the comic from its bag, beware of the tape that is used to seal the bag; if the tape sticks to the cover of the comic, permanent damage will result.
2. Gently lay the comic (unopened) in the palm of your hand so that it will stay relatively flat.
3. You can now leaf through the book by carefully turning the pages with the thumb and forefinger of the other hand. Avoid creating stress lines on the covers with your fingers and be particularly cautious about bending the cover back too far on a Mint comic.
4. After examining the book, carefully insert it back into the bag after removing the tape from the flap. If you are handling someone else's comics, it is advisable to ask permission before removing the comic from the bag, so that it will be that person's responsibility if the book gets damaged.

If this sounds like a lot of trouble, then you're not going to do well as a collector of comics, because there are many other aspects to protecting your books properly.

Storing Comics

Comics can suffer permanent damage if stored in damp basements (they get moldy), hot attics (they get dried out and brittle), or in garages (they get eaten by critters). The best

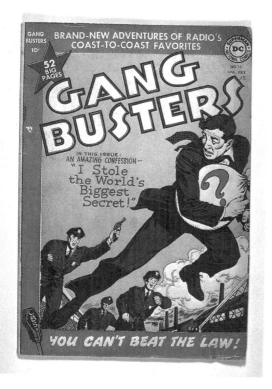

Fig. 8-1. *Gangbusters #16.* Famous radio show in comic-book form. (© DC Comics)

place to store your collection is in a cool, dry room away from direct sunlight and the ultraviolet effects of fluorescent lighting.

If you can't find a room where the temperature is a constant 65°F, then at least be sure that the air is dehumidified. Dehumidification will retard the decay that occurs due to the acidic nature of newsprint paper. If you can't avoid windows or fluorescent light, at least put up some block-out curtains and ultraviolet block shields on the overhead lights. These efforts, too, will keep the paper from yellowing and becoming brittle.

Eventually you will discover that your collection has become so large that storing it without damage is a problem. One of the best investments you can make is in proper storage materials, i.e., comics storage boxes, plastic bags, and sleeves. You can purchase these supplies from many sources, including most local comic-book shops. Two of the leaders in mail-order comics paraphernalia are Bill Cole Enterprises (P.O. Box 60, Randolph, MA 02368) and Friendly Frank's Distribution (3990 Broadway, Gary, IN 46408). Write to them for any of the items discussed below.

You should consider purchasing a supply of 3-mil polyethylene bags for placement on each comic. These bags prevent damage from dirt, moisture, and other dangerous elements that unprotected comics are subjected to. But be aware that this type of plastic is unstable and can trap the acid from the paper in the bag, thus cooking your comics in their own juices. If you use polyethylene bags, don't tape them shut. A comic needs to ''breathe'' (and you already know the many dangers of using tape around your collection).

You should also purchase some specially made and inexpensive comic-book storage boxes from you local comics shop or the many different mail-order firms that sell such supplies. These boxes do two things: (1) they physically protect your collection from light, trauma, and critters, and (2) they provide a small degree of deacidification.

Over time, the acidic content of the rag paper on which most comics are printed will cause the paper to yellow, then to brown, and finally to become brittle and crumble to dust. You've probably seen this happen to old newspapers that have been left piled up in storage. *Deacidification* can prevent most of these deteriorating effects.

There are a number of companies that will deacidify your comics, but that process can become quite expensive. It is much less expensive to do the deacidification yourself, either by purchasing and using deacidification sheets that are placed in the middle of a comic or by using the specially treated storage boxes mentioned above.

Deacidification is by no means a perfect preservation method. Damaged comics will never regain their youthful appearance, and the deacidification leaves an odd and unpleasant smell. However, it does help, and if you have a comic that is quite valuable you should probably even let an expert perform the deacidification if the fee is reasonable.

One of the best items to have on hand to help preserve your collection is a supply of Mylar bags. These tough, clear-plastic envelopes are strong enough to support your comics standing up on their ends, and the bags give off no chemical vapors over time. The bags improve the appearance of even a faded and soiled comic. Using Mylar bags also means that you don't need to purchase cardboard sheets or backing board to place in each bag as a stiffener. This will save you several cents per comic and help cover the expense of the Mylar.

Repairing Comics

All this bagging and boxing might at first seem like a lot of work, but compared to other hobbies, collecting and preserving comics is practically no trouble at all. The real trouble comes when you try to repair or restore a damaged comic.

First of all, you should never attempt to repair a valuable comic book. As you know, collectors of comics are very concerned with proper grading of a comic's condition. Each book is carefully inspected, and any repairs you perform are bound to be discovered. When this happens, the book is not only considered to be less than originally offered, but it is also considered to have been "tampered with."

On a valuable comic, it is better to accept the defect and live with it, rather than try to repair or hide it. It is possible to send your comics to an expert who may be able to improve their appearance, but if you do so you should always remember to inform a prospective buyer that the comics have been restored.

If the comic is not valuable, you can attempt to repair it yourself, knowing that the time and effort will probably not pay you back by elevating the comic's condition to a

Fig. 8-2. Acid-free backing boards and Mylar sleeves provide maximum protection for storing comic books.

Fig. 8-3. A page of original art (11″ × 17″). (© DC Comics)

Fig. 8-4. Portfolio art. A series of original illustrations collected into a protective jacket or envelope. (© DC Comics)

higher grade. In other words, your attempts to repair your comics may make them look better and make them more appealing to you, but they will not make them more valuable.

Keeping Track of Comics

The best things you can do for your collection are to take care of it and keep track of it. If you have all your books organized for quick and easy reference, you can read them with a minimum of handling. When you cut down handling, you cut down wear and tear. In order to do this, you need to have some sort of organized method of filing and finding individual issues.

The basic way to keep track of your collection is to log every issue you own into either a handwritten file-card system or a computer program. There are advantages to each.

The file-card system is simple and effective. I've provided an example of a typical design to get you started. Make multiple copies of Fig. 8-5 and within minutes you can begin to organize your comics. This system has the further advantage of providing you with a handy want list to use while at conventions or comics shops.

156

Title _____ Card ____ of ____

1 ☐	11 ☐	21 ☐	31 ☐	41 ☐	51 ☐	61 ☐	71 ☐	81 ☐	91 ☐
2 ☐	12 ☐	22 ☐	32 ☐	42 ☐	52 ☐	62 ☐	72 ☐	82 ☐	92 ☐
3 ☐	13 ☐	23 ☐	33 ☐	43 ☐	53 ☐	63 ☐	73 ☐	83 ☐	93 ☐
4 ☐	14 ☐	24 ☐	34 ☐	44 ☐	54 ☐	64 ☐	74 ☐	84 ☐	94 ☐
5 ☐	15 ☐	25 ☐	35 ☐	45 ☐	55 ☐	65 ☐	75 ☐	85 ☐	95 ☐
6 ☐	16 ☐	26 ☐	36 ☐	46 ☐	56 ☐	66 ☐	76 ☐	86 ☐	96 ☐
7 ☐	17 ☐	27 ☐	37 ☐	47 ☐	57 ☐	67 ☐	77 ☐	87 ☐	97 ☐
8 ☐	18 ☐	28 ☐	38 ☐	48 ☐	58 ☐	68 ☐	78 ☐	88 ☐	98 ☐
9 ☐	19 ☐	29 ☐	39 ☐	49 ☐	59 ☐	69 ☐	79 ☐	89 ☐	99 ☐
10 ☐	20 ☐	30 ☐	40 ☐	50 ☐	60 ☐	70 ☐	80 ☐	90 ☐	100 ☐

M = Mint / NM = Near Mint / F = Fine / VG = Very Good
G = Good / FA = Fair / P = Poor / C = Coverless

Fig. 8-5. File card/want list prototype.

A comic-book computer program has the advantage of listing many more fields of data than a simple file card. You can set up your own program from a data-management system, or you can purchase one of the preprogrammed discs available from several vendors. The computerized system of tracking your collection lets you enter and recall such additional fields of data as original cost, current market price, sale price, and quantity. If you have a computer and if you plan on investing heavily in comic books, I would recommend that you begin computerizing your collection now. Then, as you buy, sell, and speculate, you can easily scan and sort through tons of data to see which investments have paid off and which individual transactions have gained you a good profit.

Taking care of and keeping track of your comics is the first step in evolving from a basic collector into a collector/speculator. But even if you never want to sell pieces of your collection, you probably want to keep it for as long as you can. If you follow the suggestions I've presented in this chapter, there's no reason why you can't enjoy all of your comics for the rest of your life.

CHAPTER 9

Making Money from Your Investment

PAID MY WAY THROUGH COLLEGE selling comics.

I know, it sounds like an ad for *Grit,* but it's the truth. Between semesters, on weekends, and even during spring break and summer vacation, I attended auctions, followed up responses to classified ads, set up a dealer's table at comics conventions, and made enough money to afford a B.A. in the humanities.

Not that this profit wasn't taxable. Believe me, I did things right. I kept track of each purchase and sale, paying Uncle Sam for my income. Nonetheless, I got a high level of education from my dealings in comics, and I got to go to college, too!

The secret of my success is the old principle of supply and demand. I actively sought out sources for old comics and then transported them to the marketplace where the demand was high. It's a lot like farming: you plant the seed of inquiry with a word here or an advertisement there; then you work to grow and harvest your crop of rare, collectible comics; finally, you sell your produce at a comics convention or through an ad. Following that, you reinvest your profit in planting more promotions, and you're off on another round of investment. Naturally, along the way you read as many of the books as you can, so it's not so much work as it is fun!

The main thing you are after is profit. As long as you make a profit, any comic you desire can be yours. And if you have the books, all you need for profit is to know what your customers want to buy. Remember, there are three types of comic collectors: the basic collector, the speculator/collector, and the investor/dealer.

The basic collector (BC) will buy whatever looks good and is affordable. The BC will change directions and tastes quite often and, consequently, can be a source for lots of relatively new and interesting comics. Sometimes the BC gets tired of comics altogether and sells off an entire collection—for a song. In other cases, the BC evolves into a speculator/collector. Almost every regular customer of a comics shop is a BC. You should look at a BC as a resource for recent comics at affordable prices.

Fig. 9-1. *The Human Torch #2. The Human Torch* series was popular for decades, but it was toned down in the 1970s because of the fear that young readers might attempt to emulate the character's self-immolation. (© Marvel Comics)

Fig. 9-2. DC's 100-page *Adventure Comics* featuring Supergirl. The DC female superhero has had a tough time finding success in comics. Supergirl died in 1987. Wonder Woman has gone through at least five incarnations, seeking her specific audience. The Black Canary discovered that she was her own daughter, in order to maintain a 40 year continuity. (© DC Comics)

The speculator/collector (S/C) buys new comics much like a BC—except more so. An S/C has a system and buys extra comics—not to read, but as an investment. The S/C loves to try to beat the odds by guessing which comics will increase in value in a short period of time, so that these books can be turned back into the comics shop and exchanged for even more new comics.

Occasionally, an S/C will correctly choose a comic that will rise in value, but usually this is not the case, since most S/Cs are just not close enough to the facts and forces that make a comic become an overnight hit. It's possible that the S/C will trade with you, using the "two-for-one" theory. You should look at an S/C as a source for high-quality special issues.

The investor/dealer (I/D) also tries to estimate which comics will be hot and how to get enough of them to make a killing. Usually, the I/D doesn't have the interest or the time to actually read comics. An I/D sells comics to customers and buys them from publishers, other dealers, and collectors. You should look at an I/D as a resource for just about any comic you desire, but getting that comic will cost you. Of course, I/D's also try to guesstimate winners from the flood of new comics that appear each year. The section below explains how it's done.

Fig. 9-3. *Hollywood 3-D.* Combining 3-D comics with a photo-cover and suggestions of sexual entertainment, this comic could hardly miss finding its intended audience. (© Ray Zone)

Fig. 9-4. *Mystic #50.* After the adoption of the Comics Code Authority, horror comics were toned down considerably. The title of this comic, *Mystic,* evokes very little fear, as is true for this issue's cover illustration. (© Atlas Comics)

Fig. 9-5. *Tim Holt* #30. Cowboys, costumed heroes, and a touch of sex helped keep *Tim Holt* comics publishing longer than many other westerns. (© Magazine Enterprises)

Fig. 9-6. *Atari Force* #1. A comic book first. A computer game spins off a comic. (© DC Comics)

Picking a Winner

Hot new comics come from two sources: either a new and unique talent enters the field, or an established comics character radically changes. What makes *Superman* #1 or *Spider-Man* #1 so important? They both represent a major change in the field of comics. As a character, Superman brought superpowers to the comics hero. Spider-Man brought superpowers to the confused and worried teenager. Consequently, both of these ideas proved to be highly popular and both comics became extremely valuable.

But even more valuable are these characters' first appearances in the relatively obscure comics of the day: Superman in *Action* #1 and Spider-Man in *Amazing Adult Fantasy* #15. These books are representative of the really hot comics that most collectors miss because they fail to notice the significance of certain first appearances.

In today's market, you need to watch *all* the comics to spot the winners. Almost every famous comic-book artist starts out in the back of some obscure comic, becoming a success only much later. Frank Frazetta's early comic-book work was in *Tally-Ho* comics; John Byrne's was in *Doomsday+1;* and Alan Moore's was in *Warrior*. Little-known comics, at best, but today worth more than you might expect due to the premiere appearances of these noted artists.

Fig. 9-7. *Nathaniel Dusk* #1. The hardboiled private eye is a staple of entertaining comics. (© DC Comics)

Fig. 9-8. *Cosmo* #6. In 1959, Archie Comics published an entertaining and humorous adventure strip about silly spacemen. This was decades before Star Wars. (© Archie Comics)

Another method of picking a winner is to avoid what is strongly selling and watch for what's scarce. If any of today's new independent titles catches hold and remains popular, the early issues will be worth a lot of cash, because most collectors aren't buying them and most dealers aren't back-stocking them. Take your best shot; buy a good lot and see what happens in a few years. If you chose correctly, you've invested well; if not—well, you can usually get back in trade what you put into the original purchase.

The golden rule of speculating is that you're trying to buy at a cheap price something that someone else will want badly enough to pay a high price for later on. You're looking for rapid appreciation. So you need to know what critical assessments you must make when setting out to buy new comics with good investment potential.

It is extremely important to be able to recognize a key issue when it is announced. This ability involves long hours studying the comics market—talking to dealers, investors, and collectors and learning what the hot comics are now and how they became hot. You will need to establish an account with a new-comic distributor, either through the mail or directly from your local comics shop (see Chapter 3).

You should always consider the likely short- or long-term future demand of a book, because it's very important to buy at the right time.

At least half of the current popular titles are not going to be attractive to you because once a title starts to skyrocket in value, everyone will hoard it with the hope of making a profit. This means, in the short term, that the book is scarce and should sell for a small profit. But in the long term the book is plentiful, so the price will go down since everyone already owns one copy or more.

The key is to buy before a book becomes hot and to sell when it gets really hot. It also is important to know when to stop buying extra copies of the current winner and look for what'll be hot next.

Watch for the things that stir reader interest, not publisher hype. At least two-thirds of today's hot comics are associated with a popular artist. If the majority of comic-book readers in your area like a new or unknown artist, you can safely expect that that artist will become very popular across the country. Popularity in the fan market spells demand, and that is exactly what the speculator/collector is looking for. Some examples of profitable books over the last couple of years are listed in the accompanying chart.

Title	Original Price	Current Value	Age
Batman #429	$ .75	$8.00	6 months
Justice League Europe #1	.75	1.50	2 months
The Punisher's War Journal #1	1.50	5.00	4 months
Wolverine #1	1.50	5.00	9 months
Aliens #1 (first)	1.95	15.00	10 months
Swamp Thing #20	.75	20.00	6 years

Why did certain comics grow in value, rather than decline? Let's look at each example.

Batman #429 contains the death of Robin, a major character of the comic for years. This death was a highly publicized event: the story line in the two previous issues of *Batman* led up to it, and readers were invited to phone in on special 900 numbers to cast their votes to decide if Robin would live or die. Major media in America picked up on the story, and just about everyone, even noncollectors, wanted to have a copy of this interesting and historic issue. Result? The higher demand drove the price up *1000 percent* in six months.

Justice League Europe #1 was the spin-off of another popular title, *Justice League International*. It was also a first issue, so the comic quickly grew in demand. Only time will tell if it has peaked in value or will continue to grow.

The Punisher's War Journal #1 was another first issue, but the character was already selling very well in *The Punisher* comic. Like the currently popular Batman, the Punisher is a grim, lone fighter for justice. This type of hero appeals to male fantasies and is strongly in demand.

Wolverine #1 presents another established and popular grim fighter separated from his normal group of fellow heros, the X-Men. It is also a first issue.

Aliens #1 (first printing) combines the popular and established horror science-fiction film with quality art by a relatively unknown artist. However, those collectors who bought

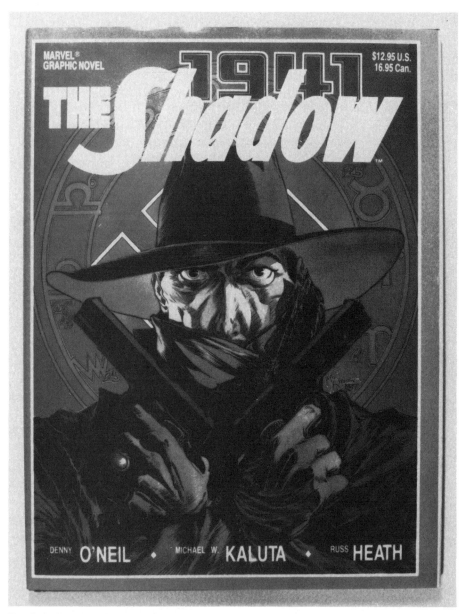

Fig. 9-9. *Shadow* Graphic Novel. The hardback, limited-edition Marvel Graphic Novel brings original material to the public for a price between $12.95 and $24.95. (© Marvel Comics)

Silverwing knew to trust Mark Nelson's art. Also, the book was published by a smaller, independent company, placing the comic outside the limelight shared by Marvel and DC. The net result of the first issue was a very low supply of a comic that quickly came into high demand. Note that the publisher has tried to sell as many issues as possible by going back on press several times to satisfy the public's demand. Still, the first printing is a part of history, and the low original print run makes this book quite valuable.

Swamp Thing #20 was a rare occurrence in the comic book industry. A writer's popularity drove what appeared to be only a plain, regular issue through the roof. After more than six years, Alan Moore's first tale of this established character still represents an increase in value of 2500 percent over its original retail price.

Basic Investment Strategy

The true art of comics investing—and any investing—is knowing *what to buy* and *when to sell*. Perhaps you should begin your speculation tasks with new comics as they appear on the newsstand. With careful management and full knowledge of new-comics trends, a very good return on your new-comics investment can be realized without a large capital outlay.

What does all this mean to the investor? It means that, unlike the collector, you shouldn't just buy what you like; you should buy what the other guy likes. The safest investment is to buy comics that have a past history of being highly collected and valued. And which are the most widely sought after comics today? Marvels and DCs. Some of their most widely collected titles include:

Amazing Spider-Man
Avengers
Batman
Daredevil
Fantastic Four
Incredible Hulk
Justice League
Superman
X-Men

Also note that the majority of investor titles fall into the following three categories:

1. Golden Age and Silver Age hero comics from 1939 to 1963, especially the World War II years and the early 1960s.
2. Disney comics drawn by Carl Barks.
3. E.C. comics and other pre-Code horror comics.

Fig. 9-10. Example of deluxe-format comic book with adult themes. Here the villain, Lex Luthor, gets all the story, while Superman is only a walk-on. (© DC Comics)

Fig. 9-11. A Canadian comic. Such comics were just as good as American comics but were never well distributed to American markets. (© Anglo-American Publishing)

Remember, too, that condition is very important. Books in Good or Very Good condition still do not appreciate as fast as better-grade comics. Ideally, your investment should be only in recent books in Near Mint and Mint condition and in books from the 1940s to the 1960s in Fine condition.

Before you invest in comics, ask yourself if you want a quick return on your money or if you can keep your money tied up for a relatively long period. If you buy comics that are good long-term investments but sell them too early, you can lose money. Similarly, it's possible to hold on to certain comics too long and lose profits by not selling them quickly enough.

You must be something of a prophet to predict the market trends in comic books. Long-term comic-book investments require you to carefully select a single issue of an older comic and hold on to it for a number of years as it steadily increases in value. It does take longer than speculation in new comics and the profits may be lower, but the risks are much lower, too.

Spotting and forecasting collecting trends is the hardest yet most profitable activity for a comic-book investor or speculator. While past trends in comics collecting cannot always predict future trends, you can learn a lot about how the comic-book market behaves if you study market activity and price fluctuations over the last several years. You'll find that slow-moving comics suddenly become more in demand, and their prices move up to adjust to the new popularity. Meanwhile, comics that had been shooting up in price will start to slow down as the price of the comics begins to reflect the true interest in the title.

At first it's better to specialize in one area, such as Silver Age Marvels or Disney comics with Barks art. You may also have an easier time advertising and selling these comics because they appeal to a special group of collectors.

A Word of Caution: Many collectors use the investment aspect of comics as an excuse to overindulge their hobby interests. You should not put all your capital in comics. Most investment specialists advise that only 20 to 25 percent of your *extra* capital be put in collectibles of any sort.

For the collector, reader, and fan who knows the comic-book field, investing in comics is a fine and fun way of making enough money to support the hobby and then some. Understanding who buys what, and when and why, can get you enough money to afford any comic you wish for your collection. And that, perhaps, is the best investment of all.

CHAPTER 10

What Is Your Collection Worth?

I REMEMBER BACK IN THE EARLY DAYS of the Silver Age of comics when I was still in high school and most of my friends had long since given up on collecting comics. Of course, I still bought, read, and collected what were called "funny books," but I did it inconspicuously.

Comics meant a lot to me then. I could "feel" the stirrings of the Silver Age with each exciting adventure of the Flash, Green Lantern, or the Justice League, or the odd and intriguing origins of Spider-Man and the Fantastic Four.

My father came into my room one evening and gazed at the neat stacks of comics resting on the shelves of my wooden bookcase. He shook his head and said, "I sure wish I had all the money you've spent on those things."

Of course, he meant this as an indication of how I'd "wasted" my cash at a rate of 10 cents per comic, but to me these comics were priceless. I knew that some of them were already rare, highly sought after, and destined to be worth much more than ten cents each. Don't ask me how I knew; I could just "feel" it. And that feeling is the beginning and end of calculating what your comics are worth.

Most collectors these days automatically refer to one or more of the available comic-book price guides to quickly and easily figure the value of their books. But before you do that, ask yourself what each comic is worth to you *personally*. Do you "feel" as if this particular issue of *Batman* is better than most? If so, then it's "worth" more to you than other issues, and you should think twice about ever selling it. Many times, the feeling is like that which you have for an old friend or a favorite toy; to other people it means little, but to you it means a lot.

Have you noticed how many times I've placed words in quotation marks throughout the last few paragraphs? I've done this because I'm not talking about agreed-upon or established things. I'm talking about perception—your perception of a "valuable comic" versus someone else's perception of a "funny book."

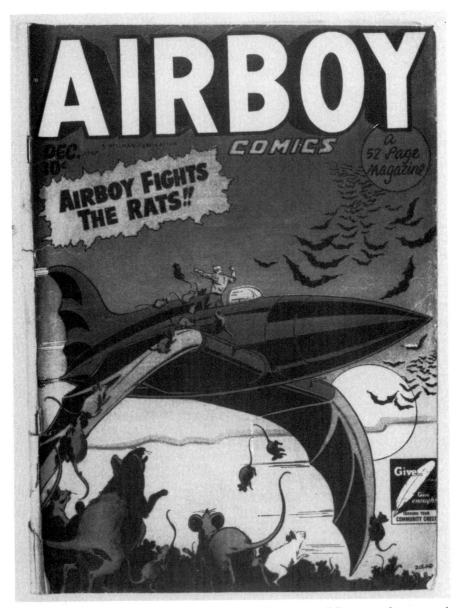

Fig. 10-1. *Airboy Fights the Rats.* Aviation comics were all the rage for several decades. *Airboy* comics combined this aviation enthusiasm with a youthful hero and a science-fiction airplane. (© Hillman Publications)

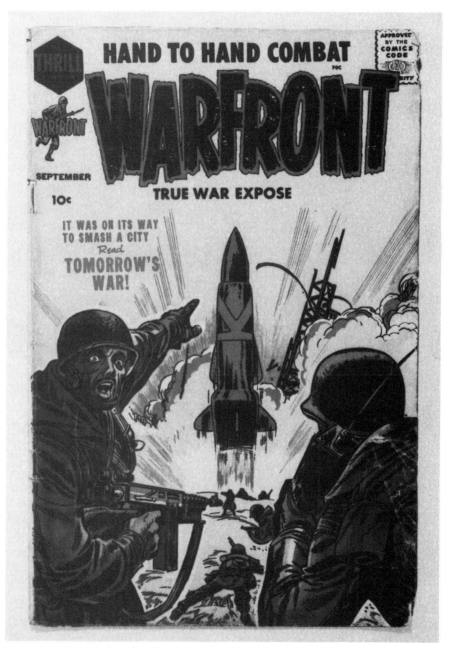

Fig. 10-2. *Warfront* #34. The cold war comes to comics. (© Harvey Publications)

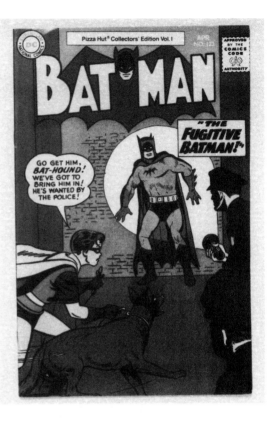

Fig. 10-3. *Batman* #123. This Pizza Hut reprint of this comic is worth only a dollar, whereas the original from 1959 is valued at $50. How can you tell the difference? Look for the name "Pizza Hut" at the top of the cover. (© DC Comics)

When it comes to placing a value on your comic-book collection, your perception will be different from anyone else's. This is because these are *your* comics, the ones you've saved and read and kept and liked. Your first impression is that they are very valuable. When you notice the prices listed in an ad or price guide, often you feel as if you were right all along to feel as if your comics were worth a lot of money. That's nice, but what good does it do you?

Once in a while, you'll be surprised to find that a comic you liked very much is listed as being worth very little. The reason is probably tied up with the law of supply and demand. No matter how much you like a comic, if there are lots of them available and a low demand, the price will stay low, too. Is your perception wrong? No, it's just different.

In the next few paragraphs I'm going to show you four different ways to value your comics collection, all based on different perceptions. But, remember that the true value of any comic is always based on your own perception. If you like it; if it brings joy to you; if it is the perfect example of a wonderful comic; then it's worth more than any guide listing. It's priceless, and you should consider hanging on to it regardless of it's accepted "value."

The *salvage price* of comics is the price someone will pay you for the bulk paper on which your collection is printed. Obviously, the person who would pay you this has no perception of comics beyond that of recyclable paper. In reference to values listed in comics price guides, the salvage price usually amounts to only about 20 percent of the lowest listing. If you sell your comics at the salvage price, you will get quick cash, little discussion, and low money.

The *basic price* of your comics is the price a retailer or wholesaler would have to pay to purchase a similar *quantity* of books on today's market. Let's say you're selling 300 comics at 50 cents apiece. When you do this you are selling to someone whose perception is of a bulk lot of comics, with little or no notice taken of specific titles, artists, or story lines. A comic is a comic, and it makes little difference to a retailer if he or she buys from you or from someone else. From a retailer you will get a little more for your collection (averaging maybe 40 percent of the lowest guide listing), only a little discussion, and a relatively quick return.

The *buy price* of a comic is the price commonly advertised by dealers who seek specific books at a rate that will allow them to pay you quickly and cover the overhead expenses of being a dealer. This is usually about 50 percent of the properly graded guide price, but sometimes it can be a little more, if the dealer or collector shares your perception that your books are special or better-than-average. The buy price assures you a good profit on your investment, assuming you can connect with such a buyer. It also assures you a rather lengthy discussion and inspection of each book and, many times, a longer payment period.

The *guide price* of a comic is the price listed in various comic-book price guides. It represents the selling price, or asking price commonly agreed upon by most dealers. Of course, you know that you can usually find comics for sale for less than the guide price, so it's reasonable to expect that you'll be asked to sell your comics at prices below those listed in the guides. Still, you usually can get something close to the properly graded guide price, if you sell or trade your books to another collector. This is because other collectors usually share your perception of a comic's value. Unless your tastes are still uneducated or completely out of line with the tastes of most comics fans, you can expect the guide price to give you a respectable return and a long discussion with other collectors of comic books. And what's so bad about that?

A final word about the guide price. You should think of it as a reference for *trading* comics, not for buying or selling. Since there are so many comics and so many perceptions of their worth, the guide price is a guide to help you swap a lot of books with a minimum of argument. Also, it is handy for figuring back to the other kinds of prices—e.g., 40 percent of the guide price is equal to the basic price.

Now you see why it was important to learn to grade comics properly as described in Chapter 6. What you know and can learn about comics will pay you back by establishing within you a sense of proper and fair pricing. This is an instinct based on know-how, experience, and your own perception of quality. It cannot be looked up in a book. Once

Fig. 10-4. *Famous Funnies* #203. Toward the end of its run, *Famous Funnies* began to feature fewer and fewer reprints of newspaper strips and more and more original stories of true-life adventures. It was a questionable improvement. (© Eastern Color Printing)

Fig. 10-5. *Master Comics* with patriotic war motif cover. (© Fawcett Publications)

Fig. 10-6. *Aliens* #1. Today's popular film is tomorrow's comic-book series.
(© Black Horse Comics)

Fig. 10-7. *Watchmen* series boxed set. Twelve issues plus end papers bound and gilded—a collector's dream. More are bound to appear in the 1990s. (© DC Comics)

you've developed this skill, you'll be able to look at any comic and fairly and honestly estimate its value.

It's comforting to know that your comics are not just "funny books" and that they'll always be there when and if you need the cash. But unless you're serious about selling your collection, it's not very important to know what your comics are worth each and every day on the open market. Just read, collect, and enjoy them.

CHAPTER 11

Selling Comics at a Profit

FIFTEEN YEARS AGO there were people knocking on my door to buy my old comics. Now I've got to knock on a few doors myself to sell today's books. Rare comics sell themselves, but common comics need to be packaged and pushed. Simple supply and demand, except for the fact that most older comics fall into a gray area between rare and common. Then, what do you do?

The Rule of One-Half

Even with comics that are 30 years old, you have to buy them at retail prices and sell at wholesale. For example, suppose you buy an old *X-Men* comic for $100 from a dealer. If you read the book and take it back to the dealer the very next day, he or she will probably be able to buy it back from you for only $50. This is the *Rule of One-Half:* You can sell a certain comic to a dealer for about one-half of the price you could buy that same comic (or the same issue in similar condition) from the same dealer.

Another way to look at it is that in order to recoup your initial investment, you're going to have to wait until the book is worth at least $200 retail before you can sell it for the $100 wholesale that you originally paid. This means you should view your comics as long-term investments, since the average appreciation of even the most steady Golden Age comic is only 25 percent per annum. That equates to a waiting period of roughly three years before you break even.

Twenty-five percent appreciation is a lot better than most stocks, bonds, or money in the bank. And many books do even better over the long haul. For example, a Fine-condition copy of *Batman* #17 increased in value between 1979 and 1989 from $30 to $180; that's an annual average increase of 30 percent. Similarly, a Fine copy of *Superman*

Fig. 11-1. *Big Town* #43. This comic was published the same week as *Western* #61 (see Fig. 11-2) by the same publisher and drawn by the same artist; the reflected killer popped up again. (© DC Comics)

#20 rose from $53 to $220 during the same time period; that's an annual average increase of 31.5 percent.

However, many "gray area" books don't always do as well as 25 percent. Surprisingly, a Fine copy of *Tales from the Crypt* #25, for instance, only appreciated at an annual rate of 10.6 percent from 1979 to 1989. You've got to be creative if you want to get money out of your collection.

There are many ways to sell your comics. Some are quick and make you very little profit. Others are long, drawn-out affairs that can give you a good return on your investment. After reading the previous chapters of this book, you should already have a pretty good idea of what to sell and where. Now the trick is knowing when and how to sell your comics.

When to Sell

Outside of someone walking up and knocking on your door, asking to buy your books at top dollar (you *would* sell under those conditions, wouldn't you?), the best time to sell is when you're not in the mood or when you're not in need of the money. When

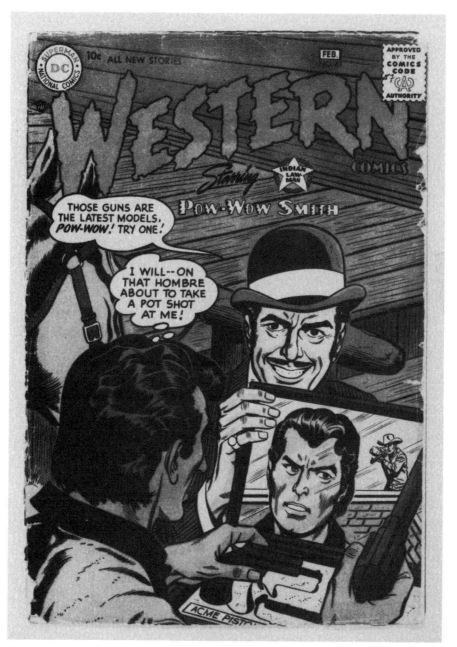

Fig. 11-2. *Western* #61. Finding good story concepts after the institution of the Comics Code became a real challenge. DC Comics implied the threat of a reflected killer in this February 1957 cover. (© DC Comics)

you're not in a hurry to sell your books, you will hold back, until a deal is strongly in your favor. A dealer does this because to the dealer the sale of comics is necessary income, but not income that should be realized at a terrible financial sacrifice.

Try to keep your *need* to sell your comics to a minimum so you won't be tempted to let the books go at below value. Like buying, if you can control your desire to rush through the deal, you stand a good chance to improve the deal in your favor. So how can you casually sell your comics? Chapter 7 explained how you can sell at conventions, and you know that you can almost always sell your comics back to a comic-book shop, but these methods are obvious and will net you only a modest profit. There are at least four other ways of selling your comics that will require a bit more effort but will get you a higher return.

Selling on Consignment

In consignment sales, you allow a dealer to keep your comics in the shop, or take them to a convention, in the hope that they'll sell more easily there than in storage. Because the dealer is not actually buying your books, you don't get paid until a customer pays the dealer. But, since you are "using" the dealer's site, as well as his or her time and effort, to improve your product's exposure to the mass market, you should expect to pay a small percentage or carrying fee to the dealer out of each sale.

The risks of consignment sales are that your books may not sell for some time (or at all); that they may be damaged while on display; that the dealer will perhaps not try very hard to sell your items; and that the dealer won't report honestly the final sale price. You can minimize these risks by working out a written agreement that includes the following points:

- Detailed description of all items
- Sale price
- Responsibility for loss or damage
- Length of time of consignment
- Date of payment

Be sure the agreement is dated and signed by both parties. You each then keep a copy, and the dealer does all the work, while you reap most of the rewards.

Mail Auctions

Golden Age and Silver Age comics are at a premium and are likely to remain that way for a long time. More and more dealers are beginning to advertise their "buying lists."

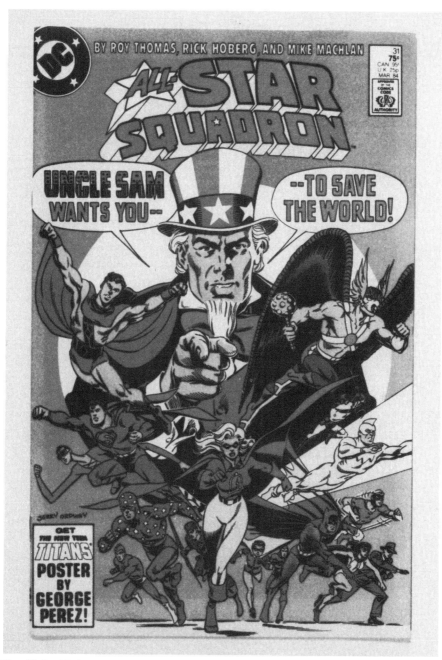

Fig. 11-3. *All-Star Squadron* #31. Patriotic superheroics in the reinterpreted history of Golden Age comics, circa 1983. (© DC Comics)

This means it's a seller's market, and you can sell almost any time you choose at any price—especially at an auction managed by a reputable dealer. Dealer auctions are not always handled by comics-shop owners; often they involve antiques dealers and managers of collectibles shops.

As with consignment sales, the main disadvantage to selling your comics through a dealer auction is the comparatively long time between the day you consign the items and the day of the auction, plus the time that elapses between the sale and the receipt of payment.

The best way to become a part of a dealer auction is to read antique and collectible trade publications and contact a number of the auctioneers to tell them what you have to sell. Several of these magazines can be found at larger newsstands.

When you begin discussing an auction sale, ask about the commission. Is it a flat rate or a sliding scale? What other costs will you incur? Insurance? Shipping? When will the sale be held? When will it be over? When will payment be made? As an extra service, sometimes auction houses can establish a minimum bid for your books so they won't sell at an extremely low rate. Ask about the details of this service and the fee, if any. Usually, all this is covered in the auctioneer's contract, so be sure to ask for a copy to review before you commit.

Running Your Own Auction

One way to avoid the delay and doubt of an auction is to run it yourself. If you do it yourself, you'll need to design an ad for publication and clearly establish the ground rules for the auction with your bidders. Your rules should include the deadline for final bids, the increase increments, and the shipping information.

Here are a few tips that will make running your auction sale even easier:

- Group all of the items in your auction advertisement into categories according to condition. For example, put all the Mint comics, regardless of title, into the same area in the advertisement. This way, the headings for each condition category save you the effort and space of individually listing the grade of every comic.
- Consider offering several like items, or a complete run of a comic, as a "lot." This cuts down on the number of items you have to keep track of and creates a bargain feeling among your bidders.
- Be sure you clearly list the minimum bid you'll accept on each item, so that you don't end up selling a comic at a loss.
- Permit bidders to call you at their expense on the last day of the auction after, say, 8 P.M. This allows a bidder to find out what the latest bid is and to top it by the stated increase increment if he or she wants to.
- Consider including a flat rate for postage per shipment. This should be an amount that will cover your costs, yet simplify billing.

All this can be quite a task, but you save a lot by doing it yourself and you gain the

Fig. 11-4. *Year's Best Comic Stories* #11, the best of DC from 1980. A variation of the standard comic format is the digest reprint of the best stories in miniature (5″ × 6″). (© DC Comics)

experience of knowing exactly what's going on during every phase of the auction procedure.

Running an Ad

The easiest and most profitable way to sell your comics is to buy space in one or more of the comic-book publications and run an ad selling directly to other collectors all across the country.

A variation of this technique might help you sell your entire collection at once. Assemble a list of dealers from the various ads you find in price guides and other publications and do a mass mailing of your list with prices to these potential buyers. Remember to carefully reflect proper grading on each item. Break the list down into lots and list a special price for each lot. It's also a good idea to give a low "one price takes all" in the hopes of selling everything to one dealer in one shipment.

If you receive a response in the form of an offer, wrap the books up and ship them off to the dealer who made the offer. The dealer's offer letter along with your original list constitutes an agreement. After your books arrive and the dealer has had a few weeks to verify the content and grading you should receive a check for the offered amount. If you haven't heard anything in three weeks, it's time to place a polite but firm telephone call.

Let's get back to selling to other collectors through a display ad in a publication. Running a display ad is about the same as running an auction announcement. Include your telephone number so collectors can call and reserve a comic before their cash arrives on your end. And if you get two people sending money for the same comic, you'll be glad you asked them to list alternates. Tell your buyers to include something like $2 or $3 for postage and insurance, and specify a minimum order amount ($5 to $10) so you won't spend days wrapping and sending out small orders.

Be sure to specify that payment be made in money orders or certified check, unless you want to wait several weeks to see if each personal check clears your bank. Expect to have to take back a few of the comics you've sold, just because of the difference in perception of grading between you and your buyer. Refund the money quickly and without hassle; you can always sell the book later.

As an aside, remember that you can buy a comic again later, too. I've bought and sold and rebought and resold dozens of books over the years. Of course, they're often not the exact same copy, but the point is that comics are everywhere, and, now that you've come this far, your access to them is very great. You can go home again. And you can read almost any comic you want after a wait of only a few weeks, if you know where to look and are willing to pay what amounts to a finder's fee. Then you can resell the comic, hopefully at a handsome profit, and you're off on the cycle again, having the time of your life.

The secret of selling well is the same as the secret of buying well: Don't worry about possessing a comic forever; you can always get it back. Just enjoy it.

CHAPTER 12

The Future

THE FUTURE IS BRIGHT for comics collecting. Each year, more and more comic-book shops open in the United States and more and more collectors come into the market. It's possible to imagine a day when every mall in America hosts a comics and collectibles shop. The color and splash of the product is perfect for impulse buying and adolescent adventure shopping. Daily high-volume turnover, plus promotion and hype of innovative books, will draw attention to comics and collecting from nearly all age groups. If you pay careful attention to smart buying and selling, you just might become the owner of one of these entertaining and popular bookstores.

Recent successful trends in the presentation of popular, larger-than-life heroes via television and feature films suggest a rosy future for superhero comics. Big-budget adventure films with lots of eye-popping special effects stimulate the average viewer to want more of this glorious fun and entertainment, and comics are a great answer. Skilled animation studios have been quick to adopt comic book characters, creating an increased interest from the children's market. The popularity of *Teenage Mutant Ninja Turtles, The Archies,* and *Duck Tales* indicates that comics are an integral part of our culture and will continue to be so in times to come.

New collecting tools and reference volumes—like this book—are coming into the market every year. New formats for comics are spreading the ''art form'' into libraries, bookstores, and book clubs.

As far as investing is concerned, even the least profitable example cited in Chapter 11 returned an average annual increase on investment of over 10 percent! If you buy cautiously and sell well, you can expect a handsome profit from this hobby right on into the twenty-first century.

Fig. 12-1. *Ambush Bug* #1. DC's most offbeat character. (© DC Comics)

Fig. 12-2. *Batman* #567. In the 1990s, comic books will feature more out-of-genre and recognized authors. (© DC Comics)

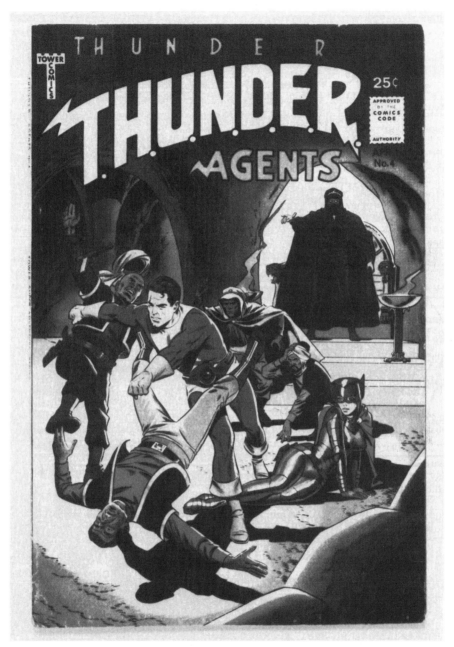

Fig. 12-3. *T.H.U.N.D.E.R. Agents* #4. The mid-1960s *Man from U.N.C.L.E.* craze created a whole new comic company under the control of Wally Wood. Tower Comics was an early experiment in creator-owned comics. (© Tower Comics)

Fig. 12-4. *Concrete* #4. Perhaps the most re-
freshing and original character of the 1980s
was Paul Chadwick's character Concrete.
(© Black Horse Comics)

Given the continual popularity of comics as a collectible, as an art form, and as a
medium of entertainment for thousands of eager, young fans, demand will continue to
increase for the comics of quality.

While none of these predictions provides an iron-clad surety, there is one thing you
can be certain of: Collecting comics will always be fun and exciting!

Resources for Additional Information

Libraries and Private Institutions with Collections

The libraries listed below maintain special collections of comic books for research purposes. They will also accept donated collections of comics material which can in some cases provide a tax write-off. Except for the Library of Congress in Washington, D.C., all of these institutions are affiliated with a college or university. If you plan to visit any of these facilities, call ahead for an appointment.

University of California at Berkeley, Berkeley, California

California State University, Fullerton, California

University of California at Los Angeles, Los Angeles, California

University of Chicago, Chicago, Illinois

Southern Illinois University, Edwardsville, Illinois

Indiana University, Bloomington, Indiana

Iowa State University, Ames, Iowa

University of Maryland, Catonsville, Maryland

Michigan State University, East Lansing, Michigan

Fairleigh Dickinson University, Rutherford, New Jersey

Bowling Green State University, Bowling Green, Ohio

Ohio State University, Columbus, Ohio

University of Oregon, Eugene, Oregon

University of Pittsburgh, Pittsburgh, Pennsylvania

College de Sherbrooke, Sherbrooke, Quebec, Canada

In addition, there are two private institutions devoted to the preservation and celebration of comics art: the San Francisco Academy of Comic Art (2850 Ulloa St., San Francisco, CA 94116) and the Museum of Cartoon Art, (Comly Ave., Chester, NY 10573).

Comic-Book Price Guides

The traditional reference for pricing information on comics is *The Official Overstreet Comic Book Price Guide,* edited by Robert M. Overstreet and published annually by Overstreet Publications Inc., 780 Hunt Cliff Dr. N.W., Cleveland, TN 37311. There are also quarterly updates recording recent comic values.

Another reference for recent changes in market trends is the *Comics Values Monthly,* published by Attic Books Ltd., P.O. Box 38, South Salem, NY 10590. The prices listed in this publication only refer to books published since the Silver Age.

Finally, every three months *The Comics Buyer's Guide,* available from Krause Publications, 700 E. State Street, Iola, WI 54990, publishes a price guide as a special section of its weekly newspaper. This guide also only covers recent comics of the last 25 years.

Periodicals

The Comics Buyer's Guide (CBG)
Krause Publications
700 E. State St.
Iola, WI 54990

> The *CBG* is a weekly newspaper full of ads, news, and features on all aspects of comics collecting.

The Comics Journal
1800 Bridgegate St.
Suite 101
Westlake Village, CA 91361

> The *Journal* is a monthly, in-depth feature magazine, providing penetrating interviews and investigative journalism in the field of comic art.

The Comic Scene
475 Park Ave.
New York, NY 10016

This slick, four-color publication is the "glamourzine" of the industry. Popular and visually entertaining.

Amazing Heroes
Fantagraphics Books, Inc.
4359 Cornell Rd.
Agoura, CA 91301

Amazing Heroes is a biweekly news and feature magazine with many articles featuring Silver Age topics.

Comics Interview
Fictioneer Books
#1 Screamer Mtn.
Clayton, GA 30525

This monthly magazine each month features four or five interviews with important comic-book creators.

The Duckburg Times
3010 Wilshire Blvd.
#362
Los Angeles, CA 90010

The Duckburg Times is an irregularly published magazine that focuses on the work of Carl Barks and Walt Disney.

Glossary

Back issue:
A previous issue of a current comic book, or any issue of an older comic that is no longer being published.

Backup story:
The first story in a comic is called the lead story and usually features the main character or is the longest story in the book. If there are any other stories in the comic they are called backup stories or backup strips. Sometimes backup stories feature characters other than the main character; they may also be shorter than the lead story.

B and W:
Black and white; usually refers to magazine-size comic books printed without color.

Baxter paper:
High-quality paper that does not deteriorate as quickly as regular paper that is used in printing some comics. Baxter paper is thicker and slicker and allows higher color contrast than normal comic paper. Introduced in the early 1980s, Baxter paper is usually reserved for high-quality, collector-oriented publications.

Big Little Book (BLB):
In the 1930s, before comic books achieved wide popularity, comic strips from the newspapers were published in a small book format. Some comics collectors also collect Big Little Books as part of their hobby interests.

Bondage cover:
Comic cover showing a female tied up or chained.

Cameo:
A limited appearance in a comic by a character from another comic, usually for only a few panels or for one or two pages. Different from crossover (see *crossover*).

Cel:
An original painting on celluloid that makes up one frame of an animated cartoon.

Centerfold:
The two center leaves of a comic, which, like other leaves, are held to the body of the book by one or more staples.

Colorist:
A person who specifies which colors are to be used when a comic book is being printed.

The Comics Buyer's Guide (CBG):
A weekly newspaper for comics collectors, edited by Don and Maggie Thompson. *CBG* is the most influential publication for readers of new comics, as well as for comic-book publishers.

Comics Code (also Comic Book Code):
The set of regulations that a comic book must conform to in order to be approved by the Comics Code Authority established by the Comics Magazine Association of America, Inc. (CMAA). This voluntary organization (CMAA) is supported and funded by the comics industry and serves as a self-censorship board. Comics that pass its standards are allowed to display on their covers the CMAA seal of approval ("Approved by the Comics Code Authority").

Con:
See *comic convention*.

Comic convention:
A gathering of fans, professionals, dealers, and collectors to buy, sell, trade, discuss, and appreciate all aspects of the comic-book field.

Crossover:
A major appearance by a character from one comic book in the story line of a different comic book, usually for several pages or the entire issue.

Dailies:
Daily newspaper comic strips.

Dealer:
A person who sells comic books, comic strips, original comics art, and related comics items.

Direct sales:
Sales of comic books directly from the publisher to the retailer, bypassing the traditional magazine distributor. Direct-sale books are sold on a nonreturnable basis.

Duotone:
Printing technique using black plus one other color ink used as an accent color.

Editor:
The person in overall charge of a comic book. Some editors only edit by making periodic checks to make sure the creative team is adhering to publisher policy. Other editors work closely with writers and artists, occasionally co-writing a story and even helping with the artwork.

Fandom:
A general term that applies to the network of all comics fans, collectors, dealers, fanzines, and all people interested in comic books for enjoyment.

Fanzine:
A specialized magazine for collectors and comics fans.

Fill-in:
An issue of a comic book done by some creative team other than the regular team; also, an issue of a comic book that does not fit in to regular story continuity.

First appearance:
The first time a comic character appears in any story or book; not necessarily the same as origin.

Flaking:
A problem with some older comics, particularly early Marvels, that occurs because small pieces of the outer edge of the cover tend to chip or flake off.

Flashback:
A retelling of a story or a character's origin within a comic-book story.

Four-color:
Refers to the four-color process used in printing in which four basic colors are used to produce all the shades used in a comic book. May also refer to a series of comic books published by Dell Comics from 1939 to 1962.

Fumetti:
A comic derivative in which posed photographs take the place of artwork panels. Popular in Europe and Latin America.

Funny animals:
A term that refers to humor and "funny" comics characters, such as Mickey Mouse, Donald Duck, et al.

Giveaway:
A comic book or pamphlet that was given away free as advertising or promotional item.

Golden Age:
A period of comic-book popularity, roughly from 1933 to the late 1950s, that saw the birth of the major comic-book publishers, titles, and characters.

Good Girl Art:
Pinup-type art usually found in comic books from the late 1940s through the early 1950s; such art was designed to appeal to young men of that time.

Grading:
Determining a grade (Mint, Good, etc.) for a comic book based on the condition of the book.

Graphic novel:
A full-length story printed in graphic album format; usually a graphic novel is an original story, whereas graphic albums are often reprints.

Hot:
A term used to describe a comic title that is selling very well or whose back issues are in demand by collectors.

Illo:
Short for illustration. May be used as a noun, such as "spot illo" for a small illustration, or as a verb, as in "illoed by Jack Kirby."

Independent comics:
Comics that are published by one of the smaller publishing houses rather than one of the major comic publishers.

Inker:
An artist who goes over the penciled drawings for a comic book in ink; the inker may often also draw the backgrounds and other fine details of a story.

Lettercol:
The letter column in a comic book or magazine.

Letterer:
The individual who letters the word balloons in a comic.

208

Limited series:
A comic book title that has a predetermined number of issues. For instance, a limited series may have only three, four, or twelve issues. A limited series is usually devoted to one popular character or concept. Such series are popular with collectors because they are easy to collect as a complete set.

Logo:
The title design on the cover of a comic book or story.

Mondo paper:
High-grade paper that is of a better quality than the traditional paper used to print comic books. Not quite as thick or glossy as *Baxter paper,* Mondo paper is nevertheless less acidic and less prone to deterioration than the traditional newsprint that most comics are printed on.

Mylar:
An inert plastic compound used for comic-book bags. Mylar is a trademark of Du Pont.

One-shot:
A special one-issue-only title, such as a collection of comic stories or a major feature.

Origin:
The beginning or creation of a comic character, usually presented in a story that details the past history of a character in the comic and how he or she came to be. The origin is not necessarily the same as the character's first appearance and does not necessarily appear in the first issue.

Original art:
The actual artwork drawn and inked by one or more artists for a comic-book page or comic strip. Original artwork is usually done in black and white (no coloring) and in a larger size than that in which it is eventually printed.

Overstreet:
Refers to *The Official Overstreet Comic Book Price Guide* prices or to the related condition-grading system.

Panel:
A single drawing enclosed within a border or frame that is used in sequence to make up a comic strip or comic-book page.

Penciler:
The artist who pencils the characters and some of the backgrounds of a comic book or strip.

Portfolio:
A collection of several higher-quality art prints, some of which are usually signed and numbered.

Pre-Code:
Refers to comics issued before 1955, the year that the Comic Book Code (see *Comics Code*) took effect. Pre-Code comics were generally more violent and more "adult" and were censored only by the publisher itself. Although technically any comic book published before 1955 is pre-Code, the term is usually applied to comics from 1949 to 1954, particularly those dealing with crime, horror, and mystery.

Prestige format:
The square-bound (perfect-bound), high-quality format.

Pulp:
A magazine from the 1920s through the 1950s that is generally printed on cheap paper and devoted to science-fiction, mystery, horror, western, romance, and adventure genres. Many comic-book writers originally wrote for the pulp magazines, and several comics companies also published pulp magazines during the 1940s.

Reprint:
A reissue of an original comic book or the reprinting of a story.

Revival:
The bringing back of an old comic-book character.

Run:
Two or more consecutively numbered issues of one comic-book title. Collectors often try to complete runs of comics, such as the first 20 issues.

SASE:
Self-addressed, stamped envelope. Usually requested by comic-book dealers when you write to them for information.

Scripter:
The writer of the comic-book story.

SF:
Science fiction.

Set:
A complete collection of a particular comic-book title, from its first issue to its last or latest issue.

Silver Age:
A period of comic-book publication beginning roughly in 1959 and lasting until the late 1960s. So called because many of the characters from Golden Age comics were revived for new comics during this period. Most comic-book historians rate the beginning of the Silver Age from the publication of *Showcase #4*, which contains the first revival of a costumed hero (the Flash) from the 1940s.

Seduction of the Innocent (SOTI):
The title of a book published in the early 1950s that details various violent and sexual excesses in comic books of that time. Comic books that were singled out for criticism in this book are often referred to as ''Seduction books'' or ''SOTI issues.''

Spine:
The left-hand edge of a comic book, where the pages are joined together. Some spines are wraparound, meaning they consist of larger sheets folded in half and stapled, while some are square-bound, meaning they consist of smaller groups of pages glued or stapled together to form a square edge.

Spine roll:
A problem often caused by the reader folding comics pages back as each page is read. The back of the spine tends to curl forward to the front of the book, making the pages no longer line up properly and causing excessive spine wear.

Splash panel:
A large panel, usually one-half to a full page, that is often used to mark the beginning of a comic-book story.

Strip:
A sequence of two or more panels; usually refers to a comic strip in a newspaper or magazine.

Subscription service:
A service offered by many new-comic retailers which enables a customer to sign up in advance with a listing of all new titles he or she wants. (Subscription service is not the same as a subscription, in which the customer makes arrangements directly with the publisher for comics to be sent to him or her as they are printed.)

Sunday page:
The colored comic strips from a Sunday newspaper; usually refers to an entire page, which may or may not contain more than one comic strip. Early Sunday pages often had only one strip per page.

Superhero:
A costumed adventurer with supernormal powers, although this designation includes some costumed characters, such as Batman, who have no powers beyond those of a highly trained normal human. The term *Super-hero*—with a hyphen—is trademarked and jointly owned by DC and Marvel Comics.

Swipe:
An imitation or even a tracing of a piece of comic artwork by another artist.

Trade paperback:
A larger paperback edition of a comic or a comic series, usually a reprint volume. Some publishers use *trade paperback* as a synonym for *graphic album*.

Underground:
Comic books published by alternative publishers that usually explore controversial topics such as drugs, sex, politics, religion, and cultural values. Underground comics are free of censorship and were originally part of the counterculture youth movement of the late 1960s and early 1970s.

Want list:
A listing of issues, usually in numerical sequence, that a collector needs to complete a set.

Bibliography

Aldridge, Alan, and George Perry. *The Penguin Book of Comics*, London, 1971.

Bails, Jerry, and James Ware (eds.). *The Who's Who of American Comic Books* (4 vols.), privately published (Jerry Bails, 21101 E. 11 Mile, St. Clair Shores, MI 48081), 1973–1976.

Barrier, Michael, and Martin Williams (eds.). *A Smithsonian Book of Comic-Book Comics*, New York, 1981.

Becker, Stephen. *Comic Art in America*, New York, 1959.

Blackbeard, Bill, and Martin Williams (eds.). *The Smithsonian Collection of Newspaper Comics*, New York, 1977.

Cavalcade of American Funnies, New York, 1970.

Crawford, Hubert H. *Crawford's Encyclopedia of Comic Books*, New York, 1978.

Daniels, Les. *Comix: A History of Comic Books in America*, New York, 1971.

Feiffer, Jules. *The Great Comic Book Heroes*, New York, 1965.

Hirsh, Michael, and Patrick Lambert. *The Great Canadian Comic Books*, Toronto, 1971.

Horn, Maurice (ed.). *World Encyclopedia of Comics*, New York, 1977.

Lupoff, Richard, and Don Thompson. *All in Color for a Dime*, New York, 1970.

Steranko, James (ed.). *The Steranko History of Comics* (2 vols.), Reading, PA, 1970 and 1972.

Thompson, Donald, and Richard Lupoff (eds.). *The Comic-Book Book,* New Rochelle, NY, 1973.

Waugh, Coulton, *The Comics,* New York, 1947.

Wertham, Fredric. *Seduction of the Innocent,* New York, 1954.

White, David. *The Funnies,* New York, 1963.

Solutions to Grading Test

Fig. GT-1.   Grade: Near Mint.

Fig. GT-2.   Grade: Near Mint.

Fig. GT-3.   Grade: Mint.

Fig. GT-4.   Grade: Mint.

Fig. GT-5.   Grade: Good. (Water spots on upper right; wear on right-side corners.)

Fig. GT-6.   Grade: Good. (Chips in upper right corner; slight roll in spine.)

Fig. GT-7.   Grade: Fair. (Ink stamp, plus chips, tears, and extra staple in center of spine.)

Fig. GT-8.   Grade: Good. (Wear on edges and on spine.)

Fig. GT-9.   Grade: Near Mint.

Fig. GT-10. Grade: Good. (Soiled cover; wear at staples.)

Fig. GT-11. Grade: Mint.

Fig. GT-12. Grade: Mint.

Index